GREAT MOMENTS OF TELEVISION

GREAT MOMENTS OF
TELEVISION

Thomas G Aylesworth

CONTENTS

Preface 7

From the 1930s and 1940s

The Early Days 8

From the 1950s

The Golden Age 26

From the 1960s

In Living Color 62

From the 1970s

The Sit-Com Comes Of Age 102

From the 1980s

Television Today 117

Index and Acknowledgements 128

Copyright © 1987 by Bison Books Corp

First published in USA 1987
by Exeter Books
Distributed by Bookthrift
Exeter is a trademark of Bookthrift Marketing, Inc.
Bookthrift is a registered trademark of
Bookthrift Marketing New York, New York

ALL RIGHTS RESERVED

ISBN 0-671-08727-4

Printed in Hong Kong

Preface

Selecting important moments in television history is not easy. What does one put in, and what does one leave out? Certainly 'the first' in any category becomes an important item, even though it might not have been a magic moment; the first soap opera or quiz show is a case in point. Then there is the problem of not being able to list such important programs as *Hill Street Blues* or *Omnibus*, since they were not the first of their genre. Then there are the 'magic moments:' certain broadcasts which have never been forgotten. And programs that opened the way to subsequent shows that are the norm today, but were considered risky at the time. There are also those programs, especially news broadcasts, that everybody saw, because viewing brought people together in times of grief, and in times of great joy.

In the main, the programs listed are network shows, since they were available to more of the American public and seen by more people. Very few of the programs mentioned were telecast before 1946, when NBC and Dumont started their network broadcasts (ABC and CBS would follow in 1948).

The list is in chronological order by date of telecast, or, in the case of series programs, by date of premiere.

Here then are the seminal television programs, both good and bad.

THOMAS G AYLESWORTH

Page 2: *Top: Hal Linden and Ron Carey in* Barney Miller. *Center: Robert Strom, the top winner on* $64,000 Question. *Below:* Star Trek *with William Shatner.*

Page 3: *Left: Ed Sullivan with* The Beatles. *Center: Senator Joseph McCarthy. Right: Sadat, Carter and Begin at Camp David.*
Page 4: *The Mouseketeers of* Mickey Mouse Club.

Left: *Top left: The first moonlanding – 26 June 1969. Top right: President John F Kennedy lies in state in the East Room of the White House. Below: Imogene Coca and Sid Caesar in a skit on* The Admiral Broadway Revue.

Above: *Left: The Wedding of Prince Charles and Lady Diana Spencer on 29 July 1981 was televised throughout the world. Right: Bob Geldof and The Boomtown Rats appeared at Wembley Stadium in London for Live Aid – 13 July 1985.*

THE FIRST TELEVISION DEMONSTRATION

It wasn't much of a show. Hardly enough to keep a movie or theater audience in their seats. But it was the first time that the Radio Corporation of America's licensees had a chance to view the product.

On 7 July 1936 RCA showed off its advances in technology and larger-screen sets for this invited group, and beamed the show over a ten-watt transmitter atop the Empire State Building in New York City. The program included speeches by three RCA executives, a production number by the 20 Walter Lily Dancers; a film of a moving locomotive; a fashion show created by the New York department store, Bonwit Teller; actor Henry Hull performing one of Jeeter Lester's monologues from the long-running Broadway success *Tobacco Road*; sportscaster Graham McNamee and comedian Ed Wynn in comedy routines and a film of US Army maneuvers.

There were 225 licensees present, plus a few non-official guests, huddled around a number of small sets in the semi-darkened laboratory. Three sets outside the lab were also receiving pictures, RCA president David Sarnoff announced with pride – and one of those was as far away as Harrison, New Jersey, near Newark.

On 6 November, RCA repeated the test, and turned the event into a gala occasion. Twenty prototype sets, ranging from 6×8-inch mirror-tops to 8×10-inch front-facing screens were set up to be viewed by 300 guests who saw a newsreel of President Franklin D Roosevelt; footage of a storm in Greenland; the Italian Army on maneuvers; music by the Ink Spots (who sang 'Mama Don't 'Low') and Hildegarde, and a Robert Benchley skit. The program concluded with a newsreel explanation of the new television procedures. This time there were as many as 50 sets outside the studio, all within the New York metropolitan area, picking up the transmission. However most of these were in the homes of RCA technicians who were monitoring reception. The days when television would be an accepted part of family life and bring events instantly to the public were still some years in the future.

Right: *Louis Hector, the star of* The Three Garridebs, *was the first actor to play Sherlock Holmes on television.*
Left: *Felix the Cat (and later Mickey Mouse) was a pioneer 'performer' on television in the United States. Felix whirled for hours on a phonograph turntable in front of television 'eyes' during reception tests in the late 1920s.*
Below: *Felix's television image.*

THE FIRST TELEVISION PLAY

The first drama on television was broadcast on NBC in 1937, when actor Louis Hector appeared as Sherlock Holmes in an adaptation of one of the more obscure stories by Sir Arthur Conan Doyle. *The Adventure of The Three Garridebs* originally appeared in the last volume of the Sherlock Holmes 'sacred writings' – The Case Book of Sherlock Holmes – which had been published only ten years before in 1927.

The adventure, which occurred in 1902, some 24 years after Watson and Holmes met, concerns a con-man who conspires to remove Nathan Garrideb, an old eccentric, from the rooms he never leaves, so that the con-man may search for a counterfeiter's outfit (printing press and engraving dies) he believes is hidden there. He accomplishes this by working on the old man's greed, in making him believe another eccentric man with the same unusual family name will divide his fortune if a third member of the 'family' can be found. The plot and the solution are very similar to the better-known *Adventure of the Red-Headed League*.

However unfamiliar the story was to the viewers, the dramatization was well-done. The critic of the New York *Herald-Tribune* noted that although the production would offer 'no serious challenge to the contemporary stage or screen,' it was 'an interesting welding of film with studio production.' The teleplay combined filmed exterior shots with live interior action, much in the same way that today's contemporary productions on the Public Broadcasting System and the British Broadcasting System mix film and video. Hector, the star, was one of the first actors to discover that televison could be profitable. *The Three Garridebs* was made during the day, while Hector was appearing in the Broadway comedy, *Storm Over Patsy*, by James Bridie, at night. He was also the first, but certainly not the last, actor to play Sherlock Holmes on television.

THE FIRST MOVIE ON TELEVISION

NBC broadcast the first feature length film on television as long ago as 1938, to the handful of New Yorkers who actually owned the primitive receiving sets of the day. The film was *The Scarlet Pimpernel*, the 1934 British classic, produced by Alexander Korda and starring Leslie Howard as Sir Percy Blakeney. Merle Oberon played his French wife, Marguerite, and Raymond Massey costarred as Chauvelin, the villainous agent of the revolutionary French government.

This adventure classic, notable for its large sets, extraordinary costumes and poorly lit scenes, was based on the popular 1905 novel by Baroness Emmuska Orczy, and adapted by Robert E Sherwood. The plot relates the story of the seemingly foolish Sir Percy Blakeney whose foppish behavior is the perfect cover for his role as the Scarlet Pimpernel, a British secret agent who rescues those who have been unjustly imprisoned by the tribunals of France, and are threatened with the guillotine during the Reign of Terror.

Howard was a perfect choice for the role of the British dandy who leads a double life, unknown to his wife. The most famous and long remembered part of the film, however, remains the fragment of inept doggerel, which comes straight from the book:

> *They seek him here, they seek him there.*
> *Those Frenchies seek him everywhere.*
> *Is he in heaven or is he in hell?*
> *That damned elusive Pimpernel.*

Also in the cast were Joan Gardner, Nigel Bruce and Anthony Bushell. The director was Harold Young.

Before long, old movies would become a staple of the network schedules, and were perfect for the extended late-night broadcasts which began in the 1950s.

Left: *Leslie Howard, at left, in the role that made him famous – Sir Percy Blakeney in Sir Alexander Korda's 1934 classic movie,* The Scarlet Pimpernel. *With him is actor Walter Rilla as Armand St Just.*
Right: *The first opera to be televised in the United States incorporated scenes from Ruggiero Leoncavallo's* Pagliacci – 10 March 1940. *In the cast were (left to right) Hilda Burke as Nedda, Allesio de Paolis as Beppe, Richard Bonelli as Tonio and Armand Tokatyan as Canio. The telecast incorporated the use of three cameras, unusual for the day, and one boom microphone on the tiny set. The vast sea of overhead lights made appearing* on television distinctly uncomfortable in those early days.

THE FIRST OPERA

The first operatic performance televised in the United States came from NBC on 10 March 1940. It was not a complete opera, but rather selected scenes from Ruggiero Leoncavallo's *Pagliacci*, with Armand Tokatyan as Canio, Hilda Burke as Nedda, Allesio de Paolis as Beppe and Richard Bonelli as Tonio. Full-length opera had been available on radio since 1931, when the Christmas matinee of Engelbert Humperdinck's *Hänsel und Gretel* was heard 'direct from the stage of the Metropolitan Opera.' The popular audience for opera was certainly out there.

Pagliacci, one of the highlights of the *verismo* style, remains one of the most popular operas in the repertoire – dramatic as a play, but gaining power through the vividness of the music. In the opera, Canio, the master of a troupe of strolling players, discovers that his wife Nedda is having an affair with a villager, Silvio. Ironically, the traditional Commedia dell'Arte play that the troupe performs echoes the conflict of Canio and Nedda, and the tension builds as the audience suddenly realizes that the performance is real. Canio kills Nedda, and then her lover, announcing to the audience as the curtain falls, 'La commedia è finita.'

The opera contains many of the most popular (and familiar) arias in Italian opera, including the Prologue, sung by Tonio, Nedda's Ballatella, and Canio's soliloquy, 'Vesti la giubba.' The networks began to broadcast operas again in the early 1950s when *Omnibus* presented *Die Fledermaus* in 1952. Today, *Live from Lincoln Center* offers the television audience two or three complete operas each year.

THE FIRST SOAP OPERA

Radio soap operas had been popular for over a decade and a half by 1946 – the first year of network television broadcasting – and TV was ready to give the audience more of them. On 2 October the first one was aired; it was *Faraway Hill* on the Dumont Network, and it was the only network show on the dial on Wednesdays, lasting from 9 to 9:30 in the evening.

The program ran a mere 12 weeks and was broadcast only in New York and Washington, but it had all the elements of the true weepy serial. Two women were after the same man, there were family jealousies, unbelievable complications and the usual cliff-hanging ending for each episode. Flora Campbell, whose Broadway career had begun in 1934, played Karen St John, a rich New York widow who moved in with her relatives on a farm, and Mel Brandt played an adopted farm boy with whom she had a love affair. Unfortunately, he was already promised to the farmer's daughter, and the result was the ever-popular eternal triangle.

Each episode began with a recap of what had gone before as well as a rundown of the characters so that the audience could keep them straight. Film clips were sometimes used to depict a speeding train or other things that could not be handled in the studio. The amazing thing was not that the show, with its cast of 16 people, was done live, but that it was staged on a weekly budget of only $300.

Soap operas found their real niche in the early 1950s, when daytime programming started. *Search for Tomorrow* began its long run in 1952, and *The Guiding Light*, which went on the air as a radio serial in 1937, moved to television in 1952. Night-time serials would not reappear until *Peyton Place* in 1964.

THE FIRST NEWS INTERVIEW PROGRAM

Meet the Press, which each week featured a well-known guest (usually a politician or a prominent government official) being grilled by four journalists, first appeared on radio in 1945. It made an easy transition to television on 6 November 1947 and has been running ever since.

The brainchild of Martha Rountree and Lawrence Spivak, who was then editor of the magazine, *American Mercury*, *Meet the Press* was billed as 'America's Press Conference of the Air.' Rountree was the moderator of the program from 1947 to 1953, when Spivak bought out her interest in the show, and she was replaced by Ned Brooks (1953-1965), Bill Monroe and later Marvin Kalb. Spivak was usually a questioner and occasionally a moderator on the show until he retired in 1975 – his last guest was President Gerald Ford and it was the first time that an incumbent president had appeared on the show.

Over the years, the program, which usually originated from Washington, DC, has featured virtually every major political figure including John L Lewis, Senator Joseph McCarthy and President Jimmy Carter in its hot seat, as well as many foreign dignitaries including Fidel Castro. Also, many major news scoops have been credited to *Meet the Press*, the news show that traces its ancestry back to the time when the entire NBC television network consisted of a mere two stations – one in New York and one in Washington. Today it is a regular Sunday fixture in hundreds of towns and cities.

STUDIO ONE

Studio One was arguably the first drama series on network television, beginning in 1948 and running until 1958 on the Columbia Broadcasting System. Actually, it was originally a radio show that premiered in the spring of 1947, before CBS formed their television network. Then, under the leadership of producer Worthington Miner, the new TV version soon became a major success.

The first telecast of *Studio One* was aired on 7 November 1948. It was an adaptation of a mystery play, *The Storm*, which had premiered on Broadway in 1929. Margaret Sullavan, the fine stage and screen actress, played the lead. She had just finished her run on Broadway in *The Voice of the Turtle*, and was one of the few prominent performers who was willing to perform on the new medium. Many stars thought that it was beneath their dignity, and many others couldn't bear to act for such low wages – often the budget for plays on television allowed a grand total of only $500 for talent. *Studio One* didn't have a sponsor to pay the bills until 1949, when Westinghouse Electric took over. Also that year Betty Furness became a commercial spokesperson on television with the phrase 'You Can Be Sure If It's Westinghouse.'

Studio One, during its decade-long run on CBS, would repeat a play from time to time, but since the earlier versions were not taped, the plays were presented in totally new productions. Marsha Hunt starred in a new version of *The Storm* in 1949. *Julius Caesar* was presented three times, twice in 1949, and once in 1955. Leo Coleman and Marie Powers appeared in Gian-Carlo Menotti's short opera, *The Medium*, reprising the roles they had originated. Other offerings included adaptations of *The Taming of The Shrew*, *Jane Eyre* and *Wuthering Heights*, but perhaps the most famous Studio One production was *Twelve Angry Men* (1954) written by Reginald Rose, and starring Franchot Tone, Robert Cummings and Edward Arnold.

Others who made early appearances on *Studio One*, in the course of learning their trade, included Grace Kelly and Charlton Heston. Jackie Gleason made a rare dramatic appearance in 1953 in *The Laugh Maker*, as did Mike Wallace in the 1955 broadcast, *For The Defense*.

Above center: *One of the early broadcasts of* Meet the Press, *obviously sponsored by Revere. On the panel, second from left, is Lawrence Spivak, the long-time purveyor of the hard news question. At the far right are Martha Rountree, the moderator, and guest Governor Thomas E Dewey of New York, who was running for president of the United States.*
Far left: *Flora Campbell and Mel Brandt in one of their tepid love scenes in the soap opera* Faraway Hill *in 1946. Obviously very little money was spent on scenery in the early days of television.*
Left: *The jury panel in the unforgettable* Studio One *production of Reginald Rose's* Twelve Angry Men *– 20 September 1954. Standing, left to right: Norman Feld, John Beal, Franchot Tone, Robert Cummings, Walter Abel and George Voskovec. Seated, left to right: Lee Philips, Bart Burns, Paul Hartman, Edward Arnold, Joseph Sweeney and Will West.*

TELEVISION'S FIRST ANCHOR MAN

NBC had started broadcasting news in 1939 by simulcasting Lowell Thomas's regular weeknight *Sonoco News* on both radio and television. But it was CBS who premiered the first legitimate network news show. Douglas Edwards had been doing television news for the CBS station in New York since the mid-1940s and, when it was decided to produce a nightly network newscast, his local show became the first network news show. At this time the official title of the program was *Douglas Edwards with the News.* Edwards continued in this job for almost 14 years, from 1948 to 1962, when Walter Cronkite took over the job. Edwards, however, stayed with the network, and in 1986, at the age of 69, he was still reporting the news on the hour on CBS radio. In 1955 he received the George Foster Peabody Award for news broadcasting.

Along the way, Edwards was often on the home screen in other capacities. He was the host of a local New York quiz show, *The Eyes Have It*, in 1948. In 1953 he was master of ceremonies of another quiz show, this time with audience participation – *Masquerade Party* – on which celebrities appeared disguised by makeup and costume and the panelists had to guess who they were. On *Youth Takes a Stand* in 1953, he was often the reporter who was quizzed by young people about the affairs of the world. He was the host of the *Armstrong Circle Theater* from 1957 to 1961 and of *FYI*, a series of documentaries, in 1960.

Above right: *Kukla and Fletcher Rabbit as they appeared on screen in an early telecast of Kukla, Fran and Ollie, one of the most enduring (and endearing) of children's programs.*
Right: *Douglas Edwards of the Columbia Broadcasting System – television's first anchor man – who began his 14-year run in 1948.*
Far right: *The stars of the Kukla, Fran and Ollie Show – Kukla (left), Ollie, Fran Allison, Burr Tillstrom.*

THE FIRST AWARD-WINNING CHILDREN'S PROGRAM

Kukla, Fran and Ollie first appeared on the NBC network on 29 November 1948, although the Kuklapolitan puppets had first been seen on TV as early as 1939 and by 1947 were regularly featured on WNBQ, the Chicago NBC station. The network show featured two of Burr Tillstrom's puppets: Kukla (which means 'doll' in Russian) – the kind, solemn, bulb-nosed little fellow with a perpetually astonished expression who knew nothing of his own past – and Ollie (actually Oliver J Dragon) – the carefree and extroverted dragon who was born in Vermont where his parents ran Dragon Retreat. Ollie was a single-toothed sentimental pushover with a terrible singing voice who couldn't even breathe fire. The only human seen on the show was Fran Allison – a former singer – who was the hostess and mother figure.

The show which was always done live, without scripted dialogue was the first winner of an Emmy Award for Outstanding Children's Program in 1949, although adults enjoyed its gentle sophisticated humor and spontaneity more than children. The program left NBC for ABC from 1954 to 1957 and then reappeared on NBC from 1961-1962 (without Fran Allison and using the title *Burr Tillstrom's Kukla and Ollie*). From 1969 to 1971 (this time with Allison) it was presented on PBS. Others in the cast of Kuklapolitan puppets were Fletcher Rabbit the mailman, Madam Ophelia Oglepuss, Buelah the Witch (named for the show's first producer, Beulah Zachary), Cecil Bill, Colonel Crackie, Mercedes, Dolores Dragon and Olivia Dragon (Ollie's mother).

THE FIRST SITUATION COMEDY

The Goldbergs premiered on television on 10 January 1949, but it had a built-in audience, since it had been a hit radio show since 1929. Gertrude Berg not only wrote the scripts but also played the lead role of Mollie Goldberg, the lovable Jewish mother who lived with her family at 1030 East Tremont Avenue, Apartment 3B, in the Bronx. After 20 years on radio, the televised version lasted until 1951 on CBS, then switched to NBC until 1953 and finally was syndicated until 1955 by Dumont – a total of 26 years of entertainment.

Mollie's husband Jake was first played by Philip Loeb, who was blacklisted in the Red Scare of the early 1950s and committed suicide. He was replaced by Harold J Stone in 1952 and Robert H Harris from 1953 to 1955. They had two children, Rosalie (Arlene McQuade) and Sammy (Larry Robinson from 1949 to 1952 and Tom Taylor from 1953 to 1955).

Mollie was a housewife, prone to gossip with the neighbor across the inside courtyard of her apartment building, always starting with 'Yoo-hoo, Mrs Bloom.' Jake was in the

Above: *A happy moment on the set of* The Goldbergs, *with Mollie, as usual, playing the benign matriarch of the family.*

Far left: *Three of the stars of* The Goldbergs. *Left to right, Gertrude Berg, Arlene McQuade and Eli Mintz.*

clothing business and Sammy and Rosalie were normal active teenagers. The patriarch of the family – Uncle David – a well-educated philosopher (Eli Mintz) – also lived with them.

When she was asked her views on the smooth transition from radio to television, Berg said, 'I've always felt the Goldbergs were a family that needed to be seen.' But, until 1953, neighbor Mrs Bloom was never seen on the show. Indeed, during all those years of radio, she was heard but once – giving out an 'Oy!' Berg explained her non-appearance: 'I'm afraid that *Goldbergs* fans have decided in their own minds what Mrs Bloom looks like, and they may be disappointed in her physical appearance.' Before the show was retired in 1955, Berg had written 10,000 scripts.

THE FIRST COMEDY/VARIETY PROGRAM

The *Admiral Broadway Revue* was unique in several ways. It was the first program to use a permanent cast that featured comedy, satire, music and dance. Several members of the cast went on to stardom, including comedians Sid Caesar and Imogene Coca, dancers Marge and Gower Champion and Bobby Van, and Judson Laire, who starred as Lars Hansen, the father in the *Mama* series, for eight years.

The show was also one of the few programs that was broadcast simultaneously on two networks – NBC and Dumont. It lasted only from 28 January 1949 to 3 June 1949 for one hour on Friday night, but was seen everywhere where there were television facilities, either live or on kinescope. Indeed, the show was so popular that the sponsor, Admiral Television sets, had to drop it because they couldn't keep up with the demand for the product that the program had spawned.

It didn't take long for Caesar and Coca to return to the small screen with *Your Show of Shows*, which ran weekly from 25 February 1950 to 5 June 1954 on NBC. It had roughly the same format as the Admiral show, but ran for 90

Right: *Two rubber faces at work on* The Admiral Broadway Revue, *broadcast simultaneously on both NBC and Dumont in 1949 – Imogene Coca and Sid Caesar in rehearsal for the show.*
Below: *Caesar and Coca in one of their zany routines on* Your Show of Shows. *This time they are appearing as Samson and Delilah. Caesar's locks are obviously ready to be shorn, even though he has not taken off his modern shoes and socks.*

minutes. Comedians Howard Morris and Carl Reiner joined the show to make up a four-person repertory company. This quartet contributed to the comedy writing, of course, but also in the writers' stable were such future luminaries as Mel Brooks, Woody Allen, Neil Simon, Larry Gelbart (the creator of *M*A*S*H*) and Bill Persky and Sam Denhoff (who went on to *The Dick Van Dyke Show*). Comedy sketches, including satires of many Hollywood movies, (*From Here to Obscurity*) were interspersed with ballet and opera sequences and became a hallmark of the comedy-variety show.

Above: *Some of the gang from the old comedy-variety program,* The Admiral Broadway Revue. *Left to right: Satirical comedienne Imogene Coca, dance director James Starbuck, dancer Ronnie Cunningham, comedian Sid Caesar, singer Estelle Loring, dancer Bobby Van and singer Mary McCarty.*

THE FIRST PROGRAM FOR TEENAGERS

Paul Whiteman's TV Teen Club ran on ABC from 2 April 1949 to 28 March 1954. Whiteman, of course, had been a musical institution in the United States since the early 1920s, with his bands, orchestras, his title of the 'King of Jazz,' his commissioning of *Rhapsody in Blue* from George Gershwin, his radio show and his movies. But this television show represented another career for him. Each week a series of youthful singers, tap dancers and instrumentalists would perform live from Philadelphia, and the winners won prizes of professional coaching and return performances on the program.

Whiteman actually uncovered some talent, such as he had done with his discovery of Bing Crosby in the 1920s. Probably the best known was a nine-year-old from South Philadelphia who joined the cast in 1951. Robert Ridarelli went on to become one of the major pop singers of the 1950s and early 1960s under the name of Bobby Rydell. There was also a young staff announcer on the program who read the show's Tootsie Roll commercials in 1952 and later went on to become a driving force in teen television. His name was Dick Clark.

Whiteman later hosted another teen show, *On the Boardwalk with Paul Whiteman*, which ran from 30 May to 1 August 1954 on ABC – another teenage amateur hour – and in the summer of 1955 he hosted *America's Greatest Bands* on CBS.

THE FIRST CHILDREN'S DRAMA

Beginning on 27 June 1949 the Dumont Network presented *Captain Video and His Video Rangers*, a science-fiction children's program that told the story of the 'Guardian of the Safety of the World' and was set sometime in the far-off 21st or 22nd century. The budget for the props used on this five-times-a-week show was just $25.00 per week, and the props showed it, but the children of the era were not as jaded by space toys as those today.

The show lasted until 1955 and Captain Video was played first by Richard Coogan (1949-1950) and then Al Hodge (1951-1955). Among the villains that the captain fought over the years were Nargola, Mook the Moon Man, Kul of Eos, Heng Foo Seeng, Dr Clysmok and Dahoumi. But the worst of all was Dr Pauli (played by Hans Conklin), the head of the Astroidal Society, an evil genius whose scientific weaponry was almost as sophisticated as Video's. Clad in a costume of military uniform, combat boots and headgear that resembled a football helmet with goggles, the captain would deal with his spaceship, his enemies and Tobor (robot spelled backwards) – the unstoppable machine that worked for the good of mankind, until it was appropriated by the lovely, but evil, Atar, and reprogrammed to 'get the Captain.'

Every episode would begin with '[We] take you to the secret mountain retreat of ... *Captain Video! Master of Space! Hero of Science! Captain of the Video Rangers!* Operating from his secret mountain headquarters on the planet Earth, Captain Video rallies men of good will and leads them against the forces of evil everywhere! As he rockets from planet to planet, let us follow the champion of justice ...'

The 'secret mountain headquarters' was filled with wonderful new devices, like the Opticon Scillometer, the Atomic Rifle and the Cosmic Ray Vibrator which made Video's enemies shake uncontrollably. Also on the side of good was Video's young sidekick, known as The Ranger, played by Don Hastings, a 15-year-old, who grew up to appear on *Edge Of Night* and *As the World Turns*.

Left: *Paul Whiteman, the celebrated band leader and 'King of Jazz,' was the host of* Paul Whiteman's TV Teen Club *from 1949 to 1954. Here he is seen with the singer 'The Incomparable' Hildegarde.*
Right: *Al Hodge (Captain Video) and Don Hastings (The Ranger) on the set of* Captain Video and His Video Rangers. *Many of the items of equipment in the control room of the rocket ship were just painted on the walls, but young viewers didn't care how tacky they were.*

THE FIRST FILMED SHOW EMMY

Above: *On the original* The Life of Riley, *Peg and Chester A Riley were played by Rosemary de Camp and Jackie Gleason. The program was cancelled after its first season – 1949-50.*
Left: *When the show was revived in 1953, it was a hit. Here are William Bendix (Riley), Lugene Sanders (Babs), Marjorie Reynolds (Peg) and Wesley Morgan (Junior).*

In 1949 the Academy of Television Arts and Sciences set up a category known as the Best Film Made For, and Viewed on Television, and awarded the statuette to *The Life of Riley*, the NBC situation comedy series. The show was perhaps a forerunner of *All in the Family*, since it delineated the problems and frustrations of a blue collar worker, Chester A Riley, a riveter at an aircraft factory, as he tried to cope with his wife, Peg, his children, Junior and Babs, and his friends, Jim Gillis and Digby 'Digger' O'Dell (the friendly undertaker). Unlike Archie Bunker, Riley was a gentle, innocuous little man and most of the show was filled with Riley's malapropisms and ill-timed intervention into minor problems. His stock answer to every turn of fate was, 'What a revoltin' development this is!'

The role had been created on radio in 1943 by William Bendix, but when NBC decided to bring it to television, Bendix had other commitments, and a young comedian was brought in to play the role – Jackie Gleason. It was this version that won the Emmy. Gleason was not very good in the role, and he and Rosemary DeCamp (who played Peg) were cancelled after the show had run only one season – from 4 October 1949 to 28 March 1950.

It wasn't until 2 January 1953 that the show reappeared, with William Bendix as Riley and Marjorie Reynolds as Peg. This time it was a success and lasted until 22 August 1958. The big reason for its popularity, of course, was Bendix, who was a natural in the part he had played on radio for so many years.

THE FIRST EMMY AWARD FOR A LIVE SHOW

In the second year of the Emmy Awards, the Academy of Television Arts and Sciences gave a statuette to what they considered to be the best live show. And, in 1949, the winner was ... *The Ed Wynn Show*. This program had premiered on CBS on 6 October 1949 and was to run until 4 July 1950.

Wynn, as 'The Perfect Fool' and 'The Fire Chief,' had begun his career of zany comedy in vaudeville in 1904 and appeared on radio as early as 1922. But this Los Angeles-based variety show of his gave millions of Americans the opportunity to see his visual gags in the flesh. Wynn's guests included some of the greatest names in comedy – Ben Blue, Buster Keaton, Lucille Ball and Desi Arnaz (before *I Love Lucy*), Leon Errol, The Three Stooges, Joe E Brown, Marie Wilson and Andy Devine, not to mention Charles Laughton and Dinah Shore.

The Ed Wynn Show was the first regular program to originate from Hollywood. It was carried live on the West Coast and, since this was before the coaxial cable spanned the country, was kinescoped for rebroadcast from New York to the CBS Eastern and Midwest networks – the complete reversal of the normal procedure in the early days of television, in which live shows were aired from New York and their kinescoped repeats were fed from Hollywood.

Although the show was cancelled after one season, Wynn reappeared in another *Ed Wynn Show*, a sit-com, in 1958.

Above right: *Ed Wynn, 'The Perfect Fool,' was the star of* The Ed Wynn Show. *His rubbery face and lisping delivery of lines endeared him to countless viewers.*
Right: *Wynn's zany sense of humor was just what early-day television needed. Here is his portrayal of a sleeping bag.*

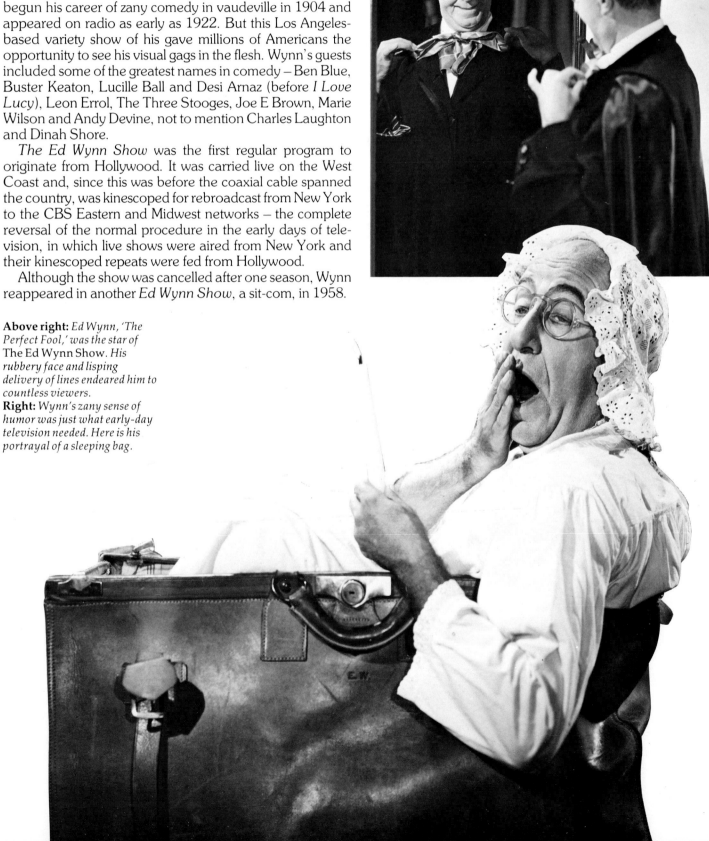

THE FIRST NETWORK NEWS SUPERSTAR

NBC began its first Monday through Friday evening news show called the *Camel Newsreel Theater* in 1948. It was only ten minutes long and had a format more like a movie newsreel than a real news show. Then, in 1949, it begat the *Camel News Caravan*, with John Cameron Swayze, an announcer who had been behind the cameras on the *Newsreel Theater*, moving from behind the cameras to the newsdesk – becoming an instant celebrity. He handled not only the news but also light features (inserted because the sponsor was nervous about not having enough visual impact) such as fashion shows (which also attracted female viewers). Swayze's signoff, 'Glad we could get together,' became one of early television's most familiar phrases. But Swayze was essentially a newsreader rather than a reporter, and in 1956 NBC replaced him with two men who had a great deal of field experience – Chet Huntley and David Brinkley. In 1960 Swayze went to ABC News, where he worked as co-anchor with Bill Lawrence and Al Mann.

Over the years he was a panelist on *Who Said That* (1948-1951), host of the documentary *Watch the World* (1950), host on *Guess What Happened* (1952), host on the

travelogue *Vacationland America* (1953), host of *Armstrong Circle Theater* (1955-1957), a panelist on the first *To Tell the Truth* (1956), a regular on *The Steve Allen Show* (1957-1958), master of ceremonies of *Chance for Romance* (1958 – an early version of *The Dating Game*), host on *It's a Wonderful World* (1963) and host of *Media Probes* (1982).

The *Camel News Caravan* was the first network news show to be broadcast in color, beginning in 1954, although regular color broadcasting did not begin until 1965. *The Caravan* ran until 1956 when it was replaced by *The Huntley-Brinkley Report*, a 15-minute newscast, anchored by Chet Huntley and David Brinkley who had first been paired during the coverage of that summer's political conventions, which in turn became the *NBC Nightly News*.

Left: *John Cameron Swayze at his desk on the* Camel News Caravan, *the program that made him a superstar.*
Below: *Crusader Rabbit and his faithful companion, Rags the Tiger, on the* Crusader Rabbit *show.*
Bottom: *Some of the characters on* Rocky and His Friends: *Rocky the Flying Squirrel, Bullwinkle Moose, Natasha and Boris Badenov.*

THE FIRST CARTOON PROGRAM

Crusader Rabbit, which ran from 1949 to 1951, was the first cartoon series made especially for television, and was the brainchild of Jay Ward and his partner, Alexander Anderson. The program came in five-minute segments and were witty episodes of a serial nature that featured Crusader Rabbit and Rags the Tiger. Crusader Rabbit was, of course, a small but noble bunny adventurer, and Rags was his less (but only somewhat) intelligent partner in his escapades. The voices of Crusader and Rags were supplied by Lucille Blass and Verne Loudin.

For some reason, the cartoons were made in color, even though color television was years away. The five minutes-length of each cartoon episode created a problem. Some stations that carried this syndicated show combined several episodes into a single weekly program, while others ran them as a single cartoon a day. The Chicago NBC station, for example, ran them in tandem with a ten-minute daily program, *The Public Life of Cliff Norton*, which featured Norton giving short, humorous talks about the problems of everyday life.

A second set of *Crusader Rabbit* cartoons was produced in 1956, but by that time Jay Ward had sold his interest in the show. He went on to develop a new series for television, the clever *Rocky and His Friends*. It is not surprising that Rocky the Flying Squirrel and Bullwinkle the Moose on the *Rocky* show resembled Crusader and Rags.

THE FIRST GAME SHOW

THE FIRST SCIENCE PROGRAM

What's My Line premiered on CBS on 16 February 1950 and was to last until 3 September 1967. During the whole 18-year-run, newscaster John Daly was the moderator.

The simple format involved contestants who had unusual jobs being asked questions by members of a panel that could be answered 'yes' or 'no.' Each time the answer was 'no,' the contestant would receive five dollars. A total of ten 'no' answers without the discovery of what the job was, ended the game and earned the guest a magnificent 50 dollars. The first contestant was the hat-check girl from the Stork Club. Each week, there would be a 'mystery guest' – a celebrity who answered the now-blindfolded panel's questions in a disguised voice in order to avoid being identified. These included such luminaries as James Cagney, Alfred Hitchcock and Howdy Doody.

The program was special, especially because the panel was always made up of witty and clever people, people who were urbane, genteel and engaging, having a good time playing an intriguing parlor game. There were four members of the panel, and for most of the run actress Arlene Francis, newspaper columnist Dorothy Kilgallen and publisher Bennett Cerf were regulars. Others on the panel included poet Louis Untermeyer, gag writer Hal Block, comedian Fred Allen and the multi-talented Steve Allen, who was the one to invent the classic question relative to the size of an object, 'Is it bigger than a breadbox?' From 1968 to 1975 the program resurfaced in syndication with Wally Bruner, and later Larry Blyden, as moderator.

Out of the golden age of Chicago television, an era that spawned such memorable shows as *Mr Wizard; Garroway at Large; Kukla, Fran and Ollie;* and even *The Breakfast Club,* came *Zoo Parade,* which began on 28 May 1950 and ended on 1 September 1957 on NBC, starring the then

director of Chicago's Lincoln Park Zoo, Marlin Perkins.

Perkins captivated his audience with his obvious affection for his charges, but his co-host, announcer Jim Hurlbut, was equally obviously uncomfortable around them, especially when the subject was reptiles. The program was broadcast direct (and live, of course) from the Lincoln Park Zoo for the first six years, ending up with two years of programs from zoos throughout the country.

Producer Don Meier came up with another idea for Perkins, who by then was the director of the St Louis Zoo. This was *Wild Kingdom*, which premiered on NBC on 6 January 1963 and ran until 11 April 1971, winning back-to-back Emmys for Special Classification of Outstanding Program and Individual Achievement in 1968 and 1969. Later, in 1971, the program, also called *Mutual of Omaha's Wild Kingdom*, was syndicated, and new episodes were made until 1978. With aid of fellow naturalist Jim Fowler, and later Tom Allen and Stan Brock, Perkins ranged the world to show animal survival in the wild, the treatment of animals in captivity, the environments of primitive people and the interrelationships between humans and animals.

Zoo Parade and *Wild Kingdom* were certainly the precursors of such sure fire programs as the *National Geographic* specials, the various Undersea Worlds of Jacques Cousteau, and David Attenborough's programs on evolution and the earth.

Left top: *Marlin Perkins, the host of* Zoo Parade, *with some of his charges from Chicago's Lincoln Park Zoo.*
Left: *Regular panelists Arlene Francis, Bennett Cerf and Dorothy Kilgallen with host John Daly of* What's My Line?

Top: *Jerry Lester, seated on chair, was one of the regular hosts on* Broadway Open House *in the early 1950s. Dagmar is seated on the floor, right, and Milton DeLugg (with the accordian), the band leader, is above right.*

THE FIRST LATE NIGHT VARIETY PROGRAM

Broadway Open House lasted only from 29 May 1950 to 24 August 1951 on NBC, but the show, the epitome of zaniness, must have set a record for forcing its stars to work the longest hours of any show – from the beginning until May 1951 it was on an hour a night, five days a week. From then on, the living was easy – just an hour three nights a week.

In the beginning, comedian Jerry Lester was the master of ceremonies on Tuesday, Thursday and Friday, and Morey Amsterdam held forth on Mondays and Wednesdays. The most famous member of the cast was the statuesque 'dumb blonde,' Dagmar, (Virginia Ruth Egnor, AKA Jennie Lewis), although orchestra leader Milton DeLugg was a featured performer. About all that Dagmar did was to wear a low-cut evening gown and read inane poetry with a deadpan delivery, but she became an American fantasy and was soon earning almost as much as Lester. Guest stars were not booked – they just dropped in to talk or perform. Amsterdam left the show in November 1950 and Lester in May 1951, then Jack E Leonard took over.

Broadway Open House proved one thing – that the American public was willing to stay up after 11 PM to be entertained by television programing. Producer Sylvester 'Pat' Weaver learned this lesson well and later refined his ideas and reshaped his concepts, introducing the *Tonight Show* three years later.

THE FIRST BEST GAME SHOW EMMY

Truth or Consequences was the first program to win the Emmy Award for the Best Game and Audience Participation Show in 1950. The program had begun in 1940 as an NBC radio program with its creator, Ralph Edwards, as the master of ceremonies. Its 17-year tenure on radio made it one of the hardiest of broadcast game shows, and when it moved to television on 7 September 1950 on CBS, Edwards came along with it. The program stayed on CBS until 7 June 1951, then had an NBC run from 14 January 1952 to 16 May 1952 and then 18 May 1954 to 28 September 1956 and 31 December 1956 to 24 September 1965, going into syndication from 1966 to 1974.

Contestants were asked a stupid question that they could not possibly answer and, when the buzzer, nicknamed Beulah, signaled that their fraction of a second time was up, they had to pay the consequences. Usually the consequences were silly stunts that had to be performed inside or outside the studio, and most of them could have been embarrassing, but, on the other hand, no one but an exhibitionist would have volunteered to be a contestant. All in all, it was good clean fun, and the show was so popular that a town in New Mexico renamed itself Truth or Consequences.

Over the years, the program was hosted by Edwards (who also developed the immensely popular *This Is Your Life*), Jack Bailey (1954-1956) and then Steve Dunne (1957-1958). The equally popular daytime version was hosted by Bob Barker.

THE FIRST EMMY FOR OUTSTANDING PERSONALITY

Nineteen-fifty was the year that the Academy of Television Arts and Sciences presented their first award for the most outstanding television personality and the winner was Groucho Marx, who was the host on the long-running NBC quiz show, *You Bet Your Life* (which ran from 5 October 1950 to 21 September 1961). Like many other early television shows, *You Bet Your Life* began on radio, in 1947.

Marx was the star and provider of most of the entertainment. The quiz aspect of the show was just window dressing. A pair of players tried to answer a few questions in a category of their choice, but the highlights were furnished by Groucho in his pre-question interviews with the contestants. The contestants could win money by answering the questions, of course, but they also could profit to the tune of $50 (this was later raised to $100) if they uttered the secret word for the evening – 'It's a common word, something you see every day.' If the word were accidentally uttered by one of the guests, a toy duck resembling Groucho dropped down from overhead. (On one occasion, the duck was replaced by Groucho's brother, Harpo.) The biggest problem on the show was the editing out of Groucho's risqué comments.

Most of the contestants who played the foil to Marx's barbed wit were nonprofessional, although a few, such as Richard Rodgers and Oscar Hammerstein II, were famous. Some, however, went on to gain celebrity, such as Phyllis Diller, Candice Bergen (who appeared with her famous father, Edgar Bergen) and William Peter Blatty (who later wrote *The Exorcist*, among other novels).

Far left: Truth or Consequences *contestant Ed Armbruster completes his consequence, the final lap of a 3800-mile transcontinental 'by land' swim as Gerry Morton looks on.*

Below: *The irrepressible Groucho Marx (right), with his announcer, George Fenneman, on* You Bet Your Life.

THE FIRST BEST DRAMATIC SHOW EMMY

The first Emmy for the best dramatic show was awarded to ABC's *Pulitzer Prize Playhouse* in 1950, which had premiered on 6 October 1950 and ran until 29 June 1951. It was then revived on 2 January 1952 and ran until 4 June that year. The episodes on this dramatic anthology program were usually adaptations of novels that had won the Pulitzer Prize in literature or drama. During the life of the program, many fine actors and actresses made their television debuts on the show. Among them were Helen Hayes, Melvyn Douglas, Raymond Massey, Edmond O'Brien, Peggy Wood (before *Mama*) and Mildred Natwick.

Great stars appeared in classic plays by such writers as Maxwell Anderson, Thornton Wilder, Marc Connelly, Edna Ferber and James A Michener, plus some original plays by such luminaries as Budd Schulberg and Lawrence Hazard. The first presentation was George S Kaufman and Moss Hart's masterpiece, *You Can't Take It With You*.

Other memorable evenings were filled by such presentations as Emlyn Williams's *The Late Christopher Bean* (27 October 1950, with Helen Hayes in her TV debut and Charles Dingle), *The Magnificent Ambersons* (3 November 1950, based on the Booth Tarkington novel, with Ruth Hussey), Sidney Howard's *The Silver Cord* (26 January 1951, with Joanne Dru and Dame Judith Anderson) and *The Happy Journey* by Thornton Wilder (4 May 1951, with Jack Lemmon).

Your Hit Parade had been a fixture on radio since 1935, and what could have been more natural than for NBC to bring it to television? It ran on that network from 7 October 1950 to 7 June 1958, and then switched to CBS from 10 October 1958 to 24 April 1959, and was revived on CBS to run from 2 August 1974 to 30 August 1974. On each show the top musical hits of the week were performed by the show's regular musicians and singers.

Over the years, the regulars on the show included many young singers such as Snooky Lanson, Dorothy Collins,

THE LONGEST-RUNNING TOP TEN PROGRAM

June Valli, Russell Arms, Eileen Wilson, Gisele MacKenzie, Tommy Leonetti, Jill Corey and Johnny Desmond. The Hit Parade Orchestra was conducted by Raymond Scott (1950-1957), Harry Sosnik (1958-1959) and Milton DeLugg (1974). Some of the best-known choreographers started out on the show – Tony Charmoli, Ernie Flatt and Peter Gennaro – and one of the featured dancers was Bob Fosse, who went on to become a fine director and choreographer.

The big problem always on the show was that the popular songs might be on the top of the charts for weeks, so it

Far left: *Helen Hayes, the great stage and screen actress, made her television debut in* The Late Christopher Bean *on the Pulitzer Prize Playhouse. Also shown is Charles Dingle.*

Above: *The gang from* Your Hit Parade. *Standing are Russell Arms (in sweater), June Valli, Snooky Lanson, Dorothy Collins and musical director Raymond Scott.*

strained the ingenuity of the staff in varying the treatment of the tunes from week to week. Some of the troublemakers were 'Too Young' (12 weeks), 'Because of You' (11 weeks) and 'Hey There' (10 weeks).

THE FIRST CHILDREN'S SCIENCE PROGRAM

A former public school science teacher, Don Herbert, was the Mr Wizard of *Watch Mr Wizard*, an educational NBC program emanating from Chicago, which debuted on 3 March 1951, running until 4 July 1965, and was revived for another season from 11 September 1971 to 2 September 1972. Herbert then returned in 1983 to begin his *Mr Wizard's World* program on the cable television channel, Nickelodeon.

Every week Mr Wizard explained the principles of science and showed how to perform various experiments with simple things found around the house. Throughout the series' tenure he had a young assistant who could be counted on to ask the right questions and would say en-thusiastically when Herbert did one of his demonstrations, 'Gee, Mr Wizard.' Also the young assistant gave the kids in the audience someone that they could relate to.

The first assistant, named Willy, was actually Herbert's 11-year-old neighbor. By the start of the 1953-1954 season, a boy and a girl alternated as assistant to Mr Wizard, thus indicating that Herbert was aware of the value of trying to sell science to females. As the show went on, the kids grew up, and naturally there was quite a turnover in Wizard's helpers.

Herbert is no longer the young stripling who made science fun, but his enthusiasm for the subject and his likeability remain undiminished.

THE FIRST MAJOR LIVE NEWS EVENT

Democratic Senator Estes Kefauver of Tennessee was the star of the first live coverage of a new event that transfixed the American public. The 'series' that was so popular that some movie theaters installed big screen television sets and sold tickets to the general public, was the Congressional Investigation into Organized Crime which began 14 May 1951. Kefauver was the chairman of the committee, and the programs were telecast live to stations around the eastern half of the country.

Probably the interest in these hearings was the result of television editorial direction, coloring what would otherwise have been a purely impartial piece of news coverage, which came at the request of the victim himself. Witness Frank Costello, a mobster, requested that his face not be shown on television. The television director obliged, and had his cameras point at Costello's nervous, sweaty hands during the tough questioning. Millions of viewers focused on these guilt-covered hands and also on Kefauver. Indeed, Kefauver gained so much fame and credibility from these television airings that he made a run for the Democratic party's nomination for president. He campaigned wearing a Davy Crockett coonskin cap, and almost succeeded.

Another television star of the organized crime hearings of the Kefauver committee was Committee Counsel Rudolph Halley who was so believably honest that he eventually became president of the New York City Council.

Far left: *Don Herbert, the pioneer in educational television, with two of his assistants on the* Watch Mr Wizard *show. His science experiments were usually done with common household objects, which made them real.*

Top: *The crime-busting Senator Estes Kefauver is seated at the table, second from right.*
Above: *A New York movie theater dropped its regular features to pick up the Kefauver hearings.*

THE FIRST SURREALIST COMEDIAN

Ernie Kovacs was a most brilliant and iconoclastic comedian who seemed to know just how to manipulate the new medium of television better than any funny man before or since. He had begun his madcap NBC show, *Ernie in Kovacsland*, in the summer of 1951, and it was on the air for an incredible five times a week for a half-hour each day. (Featured on the show was a young singer-comedienne, Edith Adams, who was to marry Kovacs and change her first name to Edie.) Retitled *The Ernie Kovacs Show*, it moved to New York and was seen weekly from 4 January to 28 March 1952 on NBC; 30 December 1952 to 14 April 1953 on CBS and 12 December 1955 to 10 September 1956 on NBC.

Kovacs pioneered the use of blackouts and trick photography in comedy. One of his shows contained absolutely no dialogue, and another concentrated on visual illusions (water pouring sideways, etc.), exploiting the false reality that only television can create.

Below: *The master funnyman, Ernie Kovacs, in one of his routines.*

He created a cast of characters that will live in dementia: lisping, myopic poet Percy Dovetonsils; German disc jockey Wolfgang Sauerbraten; Chinese songwriter Irving Wong, Pierre Ragout, Uncle Gruesome and J Walter Puppybreath. Many of his shows also included the bizarre 'Nairobi Trio,' a motley group of three instrumentalists dressed in gorilla suits, one of whom periodically smashed another on the head without either missing a beat.

The surrealist joys of *The Ernie Kovacs Show* are still available to the viewer, thanks to Edie Adams, who salvaged the rare kinescopes of those programs after Kovac's death in 1962. In 1978, some of them were rereleased on PBS as *The Best of Ernie Kovacs* and a new generation of viewers became devotees.

Right top: *Red Skelton, the superb clown, climbs the wall.*

Right below: *Skelton as Freddie the Freeloader, with Martha Raye.*

THE FIRST EMMY FOR BEST COMEDY SHOW

In 1951, the Academy of Television Arts and Sciences gave the Emmy for the Best Comedy Show to *The Red Skelton Show*. This program began on NBC on 30 September 1951 and lasted until 21 June 1953, switching to CBS from 22 September 1953 to 23 June 1970, and going back to NBC from 14 September 1970 to 29 August 1971.

The venerable comedian from Indiana – Red Skelton (who prefers to be known as a clown) – a gentle, human, funny man – had a signoff of a sincere 'God bless.' Among the characters he played on the show, most of whom he had developed on his radio show, were The Mean Widdle Kid, the chaos-causing mischief-maker whose line was always 'I dood it!'; the befuddled rustic Clem Kadiddlehopper; Sheriff Deadeye, the scourge of the West; the boxer Cauliflower McPugg; the drunken Willie Lump-Lump; the con man San Fernando Red, George Appleby; Cookie the Sailor and Bolivar Shagnasty. One new character to the television show was done in pantomime – Freddie the Freeloader, a hobo who never spoke. Oddly enough, for a show of the type of Red Skelton's, The Rolling Stones made their television debut with him.

One of Skelton's original writers was Johnny Carson, who got a big break in 1954, when he was given just a few hours notice to prepare to go on for Skelton, who had knocked himself out during a strenuous rehearsal. Carson did a great job and CBS gave him his own show in 1955 called *The Johnny Carson Show*.

THE FIRST LUCILLE BALL SHOW

It was in *I Love Lucy*, which ran on CBS from 15 October 1951 to 24 September 1961, that Lucille Ball first entertained a television audience with her antics, although she had long been a featured comedienne in the movies. No television star has endured as long as the beloved and irrepressible Ms Ball. After she was the toast of television on *I Love Lucy* for ten years, she switched from being Lucy Ricardo to being Lucy Carmichael on *The Lucy Show* in 1962. This one ran for 12 years, although both the name of the show (*Here's Lucy*) and the name of the lead character (Lucille Carter) were changed in 1968. Along the way there were such spinoffs as *The Lucy-Desi Comedy Hour* (1962-1967) and *Lucy in Connecticut* (in the summer of 1960). In autumn 1986, she returned to television in *Life With Lucy*,

costarring Gale Gordon.

Today, reruns of these shows can be seen on television at all times and at all hours. It was the great comedienne herself who said, 'I love playing Lucy Ricardo – I got to act out all my childhood fantasies.' She also was allowed to act out her real pregnancy in 1952, a television breakthrough which resulted in the birth of a son.

Also starring in *I Love Lucy* was her then husband, the former Cuban band leader, Desi Arnaz, as her band leader husband, Ricky Ricardo. Featured were the next door neighbors, Fred Mertz (or 'Frat Mers,' as Ricky would call him in his Cuban accent), played by William Frawley, and his wife Ethel, who was Lucy's best friend, played by Vivian Vance.

Left: *Ball was always willing to don crazy makeup and clown around with her husband, Desi Arnaz.*

Right top: *The four principals on* I Love Lucy: *Ethel Mertz (Vivian Vance), Fred Mertz (William Frawley), Ricky Ricardo (Desi Arnaz) and Lucy Ricardo (Lucille Ball).*
Below: *Lucy and Ethel find themselves in the middle of another fine mess.*
Right: *Many guest stars had to put up with Lucy's shenanigans. Here actor William Holden gets an accidental pie in the face.*

THE FIRST REALISTIC CRIME PROGRAM

Dragnet had two separate lives on NBC. It premiered on 16 December 1951 and played until 6 September 1959, coming back from 12 January 1967 to 10 September 1970. It was the brainchild of Jack Webb, who also starred as Sergeant Joe Friday of the Los Angeles Police Department. The emphasis on the show (which had begun on radio in 1949) was authenticity – police jargon, paper work and intensive investigation were its hallmark. The plots were taken from the files of the LAPD and every week the announcer would intone at the end of the show, 'The story you have just seen is true. Only the names have been changed to protect the innocent.' Added to the American lexicon was Friday's 'Just the facts, Ma'am.'

Friday had a variety of partners on the show, beginning with Barton Yarborough as Sergeant Ben Romero. Yarborough, however, died after just three episodes were filmed, and his replacement was Barney Philips as Sergeant

Ed Jacobs. In the fall of 1952, former child star Ben Alexander joined up as Officer Frank Smith. By the time the show left the air in 1959, Friday and Smith had been promoted to lieutenant and sergeant, respectively. Eight years later the show returned, rechristened *Dragnet '67* (later *Dragnet '68* etc.). For some reason Friday had reverted back to being a sergeant and his new partner was Harry Morgan (who later appeared as Colonel Sherman Potter on *M*A*S*H*) playing the part of Officer Bill Gannon.

Below: *Jack Webb (left), as Sergeant Joe Friday, and Ben Alexander, as Officer Frank Smith, in a 1958 episode of Dragnet.*
Right top: *Wise Men Willis Patterson, Richard Cross and*

John McCollum, with Kurt Yaghjian as Amahl, in the 1964 Amahl and the Night Visitors.
Right below: *In the 1955 version of* Amahl, *Rosemary Kuhlmann sang the mother, and Bill McIver was Amahl.*

THE FIRST ORIGINAL TELEVISION OPERA

Amahl and the Night Visitors, an opera by Gian Carlo Menotti, had been commissioned by the National Broadcasting Company and was premiered on 24 December, 1951, and has been telecast to large audiences many times since. The plot tells of a little crippled boy and his mother who live on the road to Bethlehem and are visited by the Magi on their way to see the Christ Child. Chet Allen sang the first Amahl, and Rosemary Kuhlmann his mother, a role she repeated several times.

NBC had a problem with the opera. It was a distinguished show, but the network couldn't find a sponsor to pick up the $150,000 tab. Finally they sought out Hallmark Cards, whose representatives were most impressed with the production, especially since it had such an upbeat ending – the boy, Amahl, is cured of his lameness and departs with the Three Wise Men to Bethlehem. But they quite rightly pointed out that Christmas Eve was not exactly the best time to try to sell Christmas cards on television. Then the president of Hallmark had a brilliant idea. Why not sponsor the program as a thank-you to all the people who had already sent Hallmark cards? So *Amahl* went on the air with just a brief thank-you spoken by actress Sarah Churchill and no real commercials. The NBC switchboard was swamped with congratulatory phone calls.

Hallmark was so overwhelmed with the success of the show and the good will that it had fostered that on 6 January 1952 they began the long-running *Hallmark Hall of Fame*. *Amahl and the Night Visitors* became an annual Christmas tradition.

TOKYO LONDON MADRID PARIS BERLIN MOSCOW

Above: *Jack Lescoulie, Pat Fontaine, and Hugh Downs were regulars on* Today *after Dave Garroway left in 1961.*
Left: *David Garroway with J Fred Muggs (left), and Phoebe B Beebe, on* Today *in 1953.*
Right above: *Bishop Fulton J Sheen, the cleric with the mesmerizing eyes, was a superstar of television in the early 1950s. His 30-minute weekly homilies on his program,* Life Is Worth Living, *began on Dumont in 1952 and ran until 1955, when he switched to ABC, staying with that network until 1957. Four years later, Sheen returned with a syndicated show with the same format,* The Bishop Sheen Program, *which ran for seven years.*
Right: *The present* Today *show gang: weatherman Willard Scott, anchor Bryant Gumbel, co-anchor Jane Pauley and newsman John Palmer.*

THE FIRST MORNING NEWS PROGRAM

The premiere of *Today* on NBC occurred on 14 January 1952, when host Dave Garroway faced the cameras and said 'Well, here we are and good morning to you. The very first good morning of what I hope and suspect will be a great many good mornings ... NBC begins a new program called *Today*, and if it doesn't sound too revolutionary, I really believe it begins a new kind of television.'

He then explained about how the news was written and demonstrated the world-wide coverage of news by calling Romney Wheeler, the London correspondent for NBC, concluding with 'We'll be with you every day for two hours in the morning.' And the program has done just that – occupying more air time than any other television show in history.

The studio at first was on the ground floor of the RCA Exhibition Hall on West 49th Street in New York. It had a large plate glass window that permitted passers-by to peer in at the goings-on. The crew in the beginning consisted of Garroway, Jack Lescoulie handling sports and the lighter side of the news, and Jim Fleming to take care of the hard news. In 1953, in hopes of improving the show's ratings, a new cast member was added – J Fred Muggs, a chimpanzee. His antics helped woo children, and consequently their parents, to the television screen. Frank Blair was hired to replace Fleming that same year, and he stayed on for 22 years.

Over the years, the members of the *Today* team changed from time to time, but a partial list of them reads like a *Who's Who* of television – Barbara Walters, Betsy Palmer, Maureen O'Sullivan, Frank Blair, Edwin Newman, John Chancellor, Hugh Downs, Frank McGee, Joe Garagiola, Tom Brokaw, Gene Shalit, Jane Pauley, Bryant Gumbel. The program remains as the top-rated morning show on television, although ABC's *Good Morning America* took over the top spot for a time in the early 1980s.

THE FIRST RELIGIOUS PROGRAM

Bishop Fulton J Sheen received the Emmy for being the most outstanding television personality in 1952. His program, *Life Is Worth Living* (on Dumont) had a simple format, but it was the first religious show ever aired on prime time. Indeed, it was so popular that it attracted a large audience even though it was aired opposite Milton Berle's *Texaco Star Theater* on NBC. Berle liked to joke that he and 'Uncle Fultie' both worked for the same boss – Sky Chief.'

The program began its run on 12 February 1952 and ran until 26 April 1955, and all that this charming, well-spoken Roman Catholic bishop with the piercing eyes and obvious dedication did was to tell stories and offer little lessons in morality – the words 'sermons' or 'homilies' would have been too stuffy to describe his speeches. Obviously, he wasn't able to allow sponsorship of the program, but several companies paid a premium to get their ads broadcast before or after the show, since it was so popular.

Sheen was the Auxiliary Bishop of New York and was supported by a television crew that he called his 'angels.' His famous signoff was 'God love you.'

One of the most dramatic incidents during the show's run was a program in 1953 on which Sheen was speaking about one of his favorite subjects – the evil of Communism. Looking hypnotically at the camera, he said, 'Stalin must one day meet his judgment.' A few days later the Russian dictator had a stroke and a week later he was dead.

NIXON CONVINCES AMERICA

Above: *The young Richard Nixon, running for vice-president, giving his 'Checkers' speech, broadcast from Cleveland's Public Hall over a national radio and television hook-up.*
Right: *A still from the film footage from the series* Victory at Sea *– the USS* Saratoga *burning after being hit by Japanese kamikaze planes off Iwo Jima.*
Right below: *Another still from the series showing the* PT 174 *during the Solomon Islands operations during World War II in 1943-1944.*

Richard Milhous Nixon was elected to Congress in 1946 as a representative from the state of California. He served on the House Un-American Activities Committee during the Alger Hiss case, and this brought him enough attention to be considered as a running mate for Dwight D Eisenhower. Both of them were nominated by the Republican National Convention in Chicago in July of 1952. Unfortunately for Nixon, his political integrity was called into question by allegations of improper use of campaign funds for his senate campaign in 1950, and Nixon was forced to defend himself.

Nixon chose the new medium of television to air his defense, making an impassioned speech on 23 September 1952. Having been accused of having had a secret $18,000 'slush fund,' in the face of pressure to step aside in the vice-presidential race, he denied that he ever profited personally from campaign contributions. The man made masterful use of television and was wise enough not to stage the telecast as a speech to a crowd, but rather spoke right into the cameras at the viewing audience. He evoked his wife's 'respectable Republican cloth coat' as a sign of his virtual poverty, but he did admit accepting one personal gift from a political supporter – a little dog named Checkers – and vowed he would never give the animal back. His children loved the dog, he said, and he had resolved not to surrender it. It was a triumph, and support for Nixon was reaffirmed.

VICTORY AT SEA

It was not yet ten years after the end of World War II, and the Korean War was still being fought on 26 October 1952 when NBC began its Sunday afternoon half-hour telecasts of the first news history show to gain wide acceptance. This was *Victory At Sea*, a study of the naval side of World War II.

Using thousands of feet of rare film footage from ten different countries, producer Henry Salomon carefully and painstakingly created 26 episodes following the allies in the Pacific and Atlantic Theaters of Operation. One of the elements that set the series apart from straightforward newsreel

was the brilliant score by Richard Rodgers, which was later released as a series of records. Subsequently, one melody was given lyrics and under the title 'No Other Love' climbed into the Hit Parade. The narration was by Leonard Graves.

The original broadcast which ran until 26 April 1953, proved so popular that the series was repeated several times thereafter, and was even shown on Japanese television in 1961. A similar series was prepared on the First World War and in 1974, a British production, *The World At War*, a series on World War II, narrated by Sir Laurence Olivier and featuring some of Salomon's work on the Pacific.

Salomon went on to work on *Project 20*, which produced many of the best documentaries of that era, including *The Twisted Cross* (1956), an early history of the Third Reich, narrated by Alexander Scourby, and *The Real West* (1961), a documentary debunking the myth created by Hollywood, narrated by Gary Cooper.

THE FIRST EDUCATIONAL CHILDREN'S PROGRAM

NBC premiered *Ding Dong School* on 22 December 1952, and it ran five days a week until 28 December 1956. Dr Frances Horwich, the head of the department of education at Chicago's Roosevelt University, was the motherly, slow-talking host on this early attempt to involve preschool children with learning skills. After the final program in 1956, 'Miss Frances' took the show to syndication in 1959, again helping very young children with the alphabet, arts, crafts and other activities that did a good job in teaching the moppets that learning can be fun.

The slightly cutsie title was given to the program by the three-year-old daughter of the producer of the show, Reinald Werrenrath. The child came up with it after watching a test broadcast of the opening sequence – a hand ringing a bell.

Along the way, *Ding Dong School* picked up a George Foster Peabody Broadcasting Award in 1952 for the best youth and children's program.

Of course this gentle, slow-moving program would never be appreciated by the youth of today, but *Ding Dong School* was the beginning of television's becoming aware of the importance of educating its future audience. Without it, there might never have been *Captain Kangaroo, Mr Rogers' Neighborhood, Sesame Street, Fraggle Rock, 1, 2, 3 – Go!, Zoom* or *Electric Company*.

THE HALLMARK HALL OF FAME

The Hallmark Hall of Fame has been called by one critic 'undisputably television's finest series and probably the only one in history where the slogan for the sponsor's product ("When you care enough to send the very best") can be applied, as well, to the entertainment displayed in his name.' The program began in 1952, but one of the most memorable shows on its list was telecast on 26 April 1953. It was a production of William Shakespeare's *Hamlet* and starred Maurice Evans, with Ruth Chatterton as Gertrude.

Hallmark President Joyce Hall had been keen to present some Shakespeare on television and actor Maurice Evans was eager to do *Hamlet*. But the problem was that it was hard to get a network to interrupt its regular programming to air it. No one had ever put on a two-hour drama before. Only NBC was willing to make room for the melancholy Prince of Denmark.

When the great day arrived, people all over the country tuned in, and many homes boasted of having a 'Hamlet Party,' since not everyone owned a television set, but had to view the program at a friend's house. *Hamlet* was not only television's first full-length Shakespeare, it was TV's first two-hour drama.

The production introduced stage director George Schaefer to television, and he quickly became known as a director who respected the playwright, the actors and the audience and realized all three were linked in the success of any drama.

Top left: *Dr Frances Horwich.*
Above: Hallmark Hall of
Fame: *Orson Welles (seated), in*
The Man Who Came to
Dinner. *Also shown are Mary
Wickes, Lee Remick, Edward
Andrews and Don Knotts.*

Right: *Alfred Lunt and Lynn
Fontanne in* The Magnificent
Yankee.
Far left: *Maurice Evans in*
Hamlet.

Subsequent Hall of Fame offerings included Eva LeGal-
lienne's famous adaptation of *Alice in Wonderland* (23
October 1955), Marc Connelly's *The Green Pastures*,
which was staged twice (17 October 1957 and 23 May
1959); *The Magnificent Yankee* starring Alfred Lunt and
Lynn Fontanne as Justice and Mrs Holmes (28 January
1955); Julie Harris as *Victoria Regina* (30 November 1961);
The Man Who Came to Dinner with Orson Welles (29
November 1972) and Carroll O'Connor in an adaptation of
The Last Hurrah (16 November 1977).

Like the early drama programs, Hallmark gives people
around the country the opportunity to enjoy some of the
greatest actors of our time, in some of the great plays of all
time.

THE FIRST TELEVISION EVENT

On 2 June 1953 people around the world were treated to the television coverage of the coronation of Queen Elizabeth II of Great Britain. On that day in England, the power of television came into its own. By 1953 most of the people in that country were serviced by five main transmitters, and the streets of the country were deserted, many of the shops were closed, and almost everyone was sitting in front of a television set. The cameras recorded the procession of the Queen's golden coach from Buckingham Place to Westminster Abbey, as well as the long coronation ceremony itself.

The British Broadcasting Company's television transmission that day began at 10:15 AM and continued until 11:30 PM, with an interval from 6:20 PM to 8 PM. Telerecordings were flown to Canada by the Royal Air Force and The Royal Canadian Air Force, and the networks in the United States also broadcast these kinescope recordings. Both NBC and CBS aired the film, an early example of American networks borrowing from the BBC. Using cross-Channel links, the live signal also went out to Western Europe, stations in France, The Netherlands and West Germany carrying edited versions of the momentous event.

Of course, the televised proceedings were in black and white, which meant that movie theaters were able to sell tickets to audiences who wanted to see the proceedings in color. The color feature film, *A Queen Is Crowned* was quite popular – a rare case of movies and TV working together.

Above: *The Royal Family appeared on the balcony of Buckingham Palace after the coronation: left to right: Queen Elizabeth II, Prince Charles, Princess Anne, Prince Philip.*

Right: *Part of the coronation ceremonies in Westminster Abbey, London, in 1953. The young Queen, newly crowned, prepares to receive the homage of her nobles.*

THE FORD MOTOR COMPANY 50TH ANNIVERSARY SHOW

When the Ford Motor Company decided to celebrate their fiftieth anniversary on 15 June 1953, they turned to television and produced one of the first great entertainment events using that medium. Billed in TV Guide as 'A two-hour, half-million dollar panoramic capsule history of the past 50 years, recreating in song, dance comedy, and drama famous events between 1903 and 1953,' the show, which was featured on all three networks, employed the talents of some of the greatest stars of the period.

The early days were represented by film clips from such silent features as *Birth Of A Nation*, and *The Jazz Singer*, as well as newsreel footage of great sports events. Edward Murrow and Oscar Hammerstein II commented on World War II, again using film clips for illustration. But the highlights of the show were definitely the dramatic and musical segments which included Dorothy Stickney and Howard Lindsay in a scene from *Life With Father*, and Oscar Hammerstein II and Mary Martin in a scene from *Our Town*. The great black contralto Marian Anderson sang folk songs and spirituals, and Mary Martin and Ethel Merman stopped the show in a medley of songs and duets from musical comedies including their own Broadway hits.

The show, which was produced by Leland Hayward, one of the great Broadway legends, featured choreography by Jerome Robbins, as well as a cast of more than 50, and 24-piece orchestra.

THE FIRST TRUE EXPOSÉ

Edward R Murrow's show *See It Now* was probably the most significant public affairs program of the 1950s, if not of all time. It premiered on 18 November 1951 and was the first such program to use its own film footage – no interview was rehearsed and nothing was dubbed.

For the first two years of its tenure, it was a mild show, stirring up little controversy. But then came the evening of 20 October 1953, and the airing of 'The Case Against Milo Radulovich, AO589839.' Radulovich was an Air Force lieutenant who had been ordered to be dismissed from the service merely because his Serbian immigrant father and his sister were accused of being Communist sympathizers. The broadcast created a sensation. Secretary of the Air Force Harold E Talbott ordered the lieutenant reinstated after a review of the case.

Not only did Murrow win the Emmy that year for being television's most outstanding personality, but also received a special Peabody Award. The *See It Now* show went on to win many other awards and CBS, it was said, never pressured Murrow or producer Fred W Friendly to refrain from airing any program they planned, although in the case of the Radulovich episode, both the network and the sponsor declined to advertise it in the newspapers. But Murrow and Friendly put up $1500 of their own money to buy ad space in *The New York Times*.

After the Radulovich telecast Murrow and Friendly turned their cameras on such problems as the Indianapolis American Legion's refusal to let the American Civil Liberties Union use its meeting hall; the Communist witch hunt led by Wisconsin Senator Joseph McCarthy; a report on the Supreme Court's historic school desegregation decision; a two-part series on the connection of tobacco and lung cancer (Murrow was a chain smoker and later died of the disease); and an interview with Chinese Premier Chou En-Lai. After his fracas with McCarthy, Murrow asked his audience: 'When the record is finally written, as it will be one day, it will answer the question who has helped the Communist cause and who has served his country better, Senator McCarthy or I? I would like to be remembered by the answer to that question.'

Right: *Famed CBS news broadcaster Edward R Murrow at his microphone in 1954 – the year of his confrontation with Wisconsin Senator Joseph McCarthy.*
Far left: *Mary Martin (left) and Ethel Merman singing on the Ford Motor Company 50th Anniversary Show.*
Below: *Lieutenant Milo Radulovich, with his wife, in 1953.*

McCARTHY IS DEFEATED

Wisconsin Senator Joseph McCarthy's star rose in 1950 from near obscurity into the national political sky, burned furiously for four years, and ended in decline. Few politicians ever monopolized the attention of the nation as did this flamboyant Red-hunter. Seizing on the anti-Communist issue, McCarthy dominated the headlines month after month following his attack on the State Department on 9 February 1950 in Wheeling, West Virginia. McCarthy's statement, 'I have here in my hand a list of 205 that were known ... as being members of the Communist Party,' increased his reputation as a demagogue. Growing ever more wild in his accusations and arrogant in his treatment of the president, the United State Army and the Senate itself, McCarthy led a search for Communists in the government which culminated ultimately in televised Senate hearings on ABC and Dumont beginning on 22 April and lasting until 17 June 1954.

Specifically, the Senate was investigating a dispute between McCarthy and the Army, especially over McCarthy's investigations at Fort Monmouth, New Jersey. McCarthy then declared that the CIA had been infiltrated by Communists. The Army-McCarthy hearings provided live, unrehearsed daytime drama to the viewers for weeks on end, with a climactic denunciation of the senator by the courtly lawyer for the Army, Joseph Welch. It was he who drove the final nail into McCarthy's political coffin with his question 'Have you no sense of decency, sir? At long last, have you left no sense of decency?'

Below: *McCarthy (left) with lawyer Roy Cohen.*

Right: *Senator Joseph McCarthy (in glasses at center table) surrounded by correspondents during the Army-McCarthy hearings.*

THE FIRST LATE NIGHT TALK SHOW

On 27 September 1954 the NBC cameras zoomed in on Steve Allen, who announced the beginning of the first network *Tonight* show: 'This is sort of a mild little show. I don't expect you to say, "Boy! What a program." No, just look at it and decide in about a week what you think of it. It's not a spectacular. It's going to be kind of a monotonous ... This theater, I think it sleeps about 800 people.' Allen would play the piano; talk about anything that interested him; chat with Gene Rayburn, the announcer, and Skitch Henderson, the orchestra leader; talk with people in the audience; and do funny remotes outside the studio. When he left to do a prime time series in 1956, Ernie Kovacs took over.

Then came *The Jack Paar Show* in the same time slot. Paar debuted on 29 July 1957, introduced by veteran movie character actor Franklin Pangborn, and announcing 'This is an hour and 45 minutes a night and I can't figure it out. Really, it's a telethon, but I can't figure who it's for.' The format was still simple – it was almost entirely a talk show, and some of the more or less regular guests were comedienne Dody Goodman, hostess Elsa Maxwell, humorist Alexander King, singer Genevieve, writer Jack Douglas, actor Hans Conreid, comedienne Peggy Cass, Zsa Zsa Gabor and comedian Cliff (Charley Weaver) Arquette.

But it was Paar's emotional outbursts that kept the viewers glued to their sets. At any time, Paar would start an argument with one of his guests (it seemed as if announcer Hugh Down and band leader José Melis were immune), or burst into tears when something sad was referred to. Paar also seemed to be constantly involved in feuds with other show business personalities – among them Steve Allen, Dorothy Kilgallen, Walter Winchell and Ed Sullivan.

On 11 February 1960 Paar announced his retirement from the show (although he did return a month later). The previous night he had taped the show, which included a slightly off-color story (off-color in 1960, but certainly not today) about an English woman asking about the hours of

Above right: *A kinescope picture taken on 11 February 1960, showing television talk show host Jack Paar rising from his chair to leave his top-rated NBC show following his dramatic, tear-filled diatribe over the network's decision to remove a joke from his previous night's version of* The Jack Paar Show.
Right: *Steve Allen (left) doing a Hawaiian skit with his band leader and second banana, Skitch Henderson, on the* Tonight *show in the mid-1950s.*
Top far right: *An early* The Tonight Show Starring Johnny Carson. *Carson, at the table, converses with announcer Ed McMahon, actor/singer Richard Kiley, and writer/actress/raconteur Selma Diamond.*

the WC in Europe. A man, thinking she referred to 'Wayside Chapels,' told her that they were open once a week. The network cut the story without telling Paar, and Paar resigned in tears. His final show was 30 March 1962.

Finally came the *Tonight Show Starring Johnny Carson* on 2 October 1962 – a full-fledged, megabuck variety show – quite a departure from the original *Tonight* Show. The calm and unflappable Carson put a new face on the *Tonight* show – avoiding controversy and having fun with his guests rather than making the show an emotional experience. He aimed for the chuckle instead of the tears or the belly laughs and turned the program into one of NBC's top money makers. Carson has had many imitators over the years, but in his twenty-fifth season no one has come close to dislodging the king of late-night television.

THE FIRST BIG MONEY QUIZ SHOW

Above: *Charles Lincoln Van Doren, the Columbia University English instructor who won $129,000 on the* Twenty-One *quiz show, contemplates his answer in the 'isolation booth.' He has 11 seconds to respond.*

Long before television, there had been a radio show called *The $64 Question*, and that sum was a fortune in the depression days. Then, on 7 June 1955, came CBS's *The $64,000 Question*, which heralded a new era that extolled greed. A contestant, certifiably an expert in a given area of knowledge, would be asked complex questions on his or her specialty. After answering ten questions correctly, the

contestant had won $4000, and could either take it and go home or return the next week for another question worth $8000. A returning contestant was placed in an isolation booth each week that he or she returned, asked a progressively more difficult question, and, if he or she survived, it was $16,000, then $32,000 and finally $64,000.

The program, which was hosted by Hal March, continued until 2 November 1958, and was so popular that it spawned several imitators – all offering big payoffs, such as *Twenty-One, The Big Surprise* and *The $64,000 Challenge*. Among the unlikely contestants who went home with the top prize were Jockey Billy Pearson, whose subject was art; Marine Captain Richard S McCutchen, whose subject was gastronomy; and 11-year-old Robert Strom, whose subject was science. Two people who were to go on to careers in television won the top prize: Barbara Feldon (who starred in commercials before becoming Agent 99 on *Get Smart*), whose subject was Shakespeare; and Dr Joyce Brothers, whose subject was boxing.

At the height of the big-time game show mania, the bubble burst. It all began when a standby contestant on a show called *Dotto*, Edward Hilgemeier, found some notes containing answers to the questions to be asked that were left behind by another contestant. Hilgemeier aired his find in August of 1958, and the investigations began. The New York District Attorney eventually paraded 150 witnesses before a grand jury (he later said that at least 100 of them had lied) and finally it came out that many of the shows, indeed, had been rigged, many of the producers having opted for entertainment rather than honesty. The House of Representatives Special Subcommittee on Legislative Oversight got into the act, and the public uproar forced the cancellation of most of the quiz shows (including some honest ones) and Louis Cowan, CBS's television network president was force to resign.

Probably the hardest hit was Charles Lincoln Van Doren, an appealing under-thirty English instructor at Columbia University. After 14 weeks on the *Twenty-One* show, the $4000 per year teacher had won $129,000, and was well on his way to becoming the first American intellectual folk hero, even being signed to appear as resident guru on the *Today* show. Van Doren first denied the charges, but later was forced to admit that he had taken part in the rigging. He lost his job on *Today* and was relieved of his teaching post.

THE FIRST ADULT WESTERN

Up until 1955, the Western programs on television were pretty much for the kids and starred old-time movie heroes such as The Lone Ranger and Hopalong Cassidy. Then came *Gunsmoke* on 10 September 1955, and the rest is history. *Gunsmoke* lasted until 1 September 1975, and was not only the first adult Western, but also television's longest-running Western and television's longest-running prime time series with continuing characters.

The program got its start on radio in the spring of 1952 with William Conrad (later to be the star of *Cannon*) playing the part of Marshall Matt Dillon of Dodge City, Kansas, 'the first man they look for, and the last they want to see.' When CBS brought the show to television, they took John Wayne's advice and hired the young James Arness for the role. The thing that made the series unique was that often real social issues were attacked and the characters, both good and bad, were human beings. Even Dillon was fallible.

Joining Arness in the original cast were Amanda Blake as Kitty Russell, owner of the Long Branch Saloon; Dennis Weaver as Chester B Goode, Dillon's gimpy-legged deputy; and Milburn Stone as the crusty but kindly physician, Galen 'Doc' Adams. Former Frankenstein's monster Glenn Strange played the bartender, Sam.

Weaver left the show in 1964 and Blake in 1974. But other actors filled the void – Ken Curtis as the new deputy, Festus Haggen (1964-1975), Burt Reynolds as blacksmith Quint Asper (1962-1965), and Roger Ewing as Dodge City townsman Clayton Thaddeus 'Thad' Greenwood (1965-1967).

The western setting was gritty and believable, with an attempt to portray the hardships and harshness involved in the settling of the American West. It was a far cry from the sequins and buckskins of Roy Rogers and Dale Evans, or such singing cowboys as Gene Autry.

THE FIRST WALT DISNEY CHILDREN'S PROGRAM

The Mickey Mouse Club began on ABC on 3 October 1955 and lasted until 24 September 1959, only to be revived in 1977 as *The New Mickey Mouse Club* in syndication. The original show was seen for an hour five times a week during its first two seasons and was trimmed to a half-hour in 1957. The stars were children – T-shirted and mouse-hatted – called The Mouseketeers. There were also two adults on the show – Jimmie Dodd, an actor and songwriter, who was the host, and Roy Williams (The Big Mooseketeer), a Disney writer and animator.

Most episodes featured a newsreel or other short documentary film, a production number or sketch, an episode of a specially-made film serial and a Disney cartoon. Each day of the week had a different theme. Monday was 'Fun with Music Day,' Tuesday was 'Guest Star Day,' Wednesday was 'Anything Can Happen Day,' Thursday was 'Circus Day' and Friday was 'Talent Roundup Day.'

Several Mouseketeers went on to pursue show business careers. Among them were Annette Funicello (the heroine of all those beach-blanket films), Paul Peterson (*The Donna Reed Show*) and Don Agrati (who changed his name to Don Grady for *My Three Sons*). Also playing Mouseketeers were Tim and Mickey Rooney Jr – two sons of Mickey Rooney. The Mouseketeer hats are still available.

Left: *Jimmie Dodd (left), the actor and singer, was the host on* The Mickey Mouse Club *in the 1950s. With him are Mouseketeers Judy Harriet, Annette Funicello and Darlene Gillespie. Funicello went on to star in several bathing-suited teenage movies, and later appeared as a young matron on peanut butter commercials.*
Right: *Four of the stars of the* Gunsmoke *television series: James Arness, as Marshal Matt Dillon of Dodge City; Amanda Blake as Kitty Russell, the owner of the Long Branch Saloon; Milburn Stone as Dr Galen 'Doc' Adams; and Dennis Weaver, as deputy Chester B Goode.*

ED SULLIVAN WITH ELVIS PRESLEY

Left: *Elvis Presley at work.* **Above:** *Ed Sullivan, the host.*

Many a superstar got his or her start on *The Ed Sullivan Show* on CBS, and every actor in New York badgered his agent to get him a spot on the program. Some of those who made their first television appearances with Ed were Jack Benny, Humphrey Bogart, Maria Callas, Jackie Gleason, The Beatles, Charles Laughton, Bob Hope, Lena Horne, Dean Martin and Jerry Lewis, Dinah Shore, Eddie Fisher and Walt Disney. Sullivan also featured many international acts on the show including the Moiseyev Dancers from the USSR and 'the Little Italian Mouse, Topo Gigio.'

When Elvis 'The Pelvis' Presley, the man who was to become a legend of rock 'n' roll, with a following that has made him an icon even after death, appeared on Sullivan's show, the country held its breath. Would the cameras pick up his lascivious, sensual hip and leg movements or not? In fact, on the first two appearances they did. Presley appeared on 9 September 1956 and sang 'Don't Be Cruel' and 'Love Me Tender' as well as 'Reddy Teddy' and 'Hound Dog.' On 28 October, he appeared again. It was only on the last appearance on 6 January 1957, that the cameras showed him from the waist up, in tight closeups, so as not to offend the audience at home.

The September appearance on the Sullivan program was not, as many believe, Presley's first gig on the tube, for he had made his debut 28 January 1956 on *Stage Show*, a variety program hosted by Tommy and Jimmy Dorsey. However, it was the Sullivan show that made the headlines, and Presley's appearance just at the moment he was revolutionizing popular music did just that.

THE FIRST ORIGINAL TELEVISION MUSICAL

When CBS decided to do what NBC had done in 1951 by commissioning an opera from Gian Carlo Menotti (*Amahl and the Night Visitors*), they went right to the top and commissioned an operetta by the two masters of the genre, Richard Rodgers and Oscar Hammerstein II. Those were the two who had brought *Oklahoma!, Carousel, South Pacific* and *The King and I* to the Broadway stage. It was decided that the operetta tell the story of Cinderella, in order to appeal to both adults and children in the audience.

The network also went to the top when it came to casting. The title role was to be played and sung by Julie Andrews, who had been setting Broadway on its ear as Eliza Doolittle in Lerner and Loewe's *My Fair Lady*. Also in the cast were Jon Cypher (later known as Chief Daniels of *Hill Street*

Blues) as Prince Charming and Howard Lindsay and Dorothy Stickney as his parents, the King and Queen. Edie Adams played the Fairy Godmother.

Cinderella was telecast on 31 March 1957, and was a smash hit, charming children of all ages. Some of the almost-forgotten songs (none of them became hits) were 'In My Own Little Corner,' 'Do I Love You Because You're Beautiful?' and 'Ten Minutes Ago.'

Unfortunately, the telecast was doomed to obscurity. Naturally it was done in black and white, and, since this was in the days before video tape, was available only on kinescope. Eight years later it was remade in color, starring Lesley Ann Warren, with Walter Pidgeon and Ginger Rogers as the King and Queen.

THE LONGEST-RUNNING TEEN PROGRAM

The longest-running program of any sort on the ABC network is *American Bandstand*, which began on 5 August 1957 and is still going strong. Actually, the program dates back to 1952, when it was a local Philadelphia show called *Bandstand*, hosted by Bob Horn. The set was built like a record shop and the program featured records, film clips of popular singers and live audiences of teenagers who would get up and dance. In 1956, a local Philadelphia disc jockey, Dick Clark, took over as master of ceremonies and the ever-youthful Clark has been at the helm ever since.

When it began on the network, the show was 90 minutes long, and for six years it emanated from WFIL-TV in Philadelphia. Clark kept things simple, using a set of bleachers for

the dancing kids to rest on, a podium for himself, an autograph table for guest stars and a sign showing the week's top ten hit records.

Over the years almost every famous rock star has been a guest on the program – except for Elvis Presley and Rick Nelson. In 1957 two schoolboys who called themselves Tom and Jerry made their debut singing their own song, 'Hey, Schoolgirl.' They went on to become Paul Simon and Art Garfunkel. Of course all the big Philadelphia singing stars made frequent appearances – Frankie Avalon, Bobby Rydell, Chubby Checker, Fabian and James Darren. *American Bandstand*, which moved to Los Angeles in 1964, played a part in the creation of rock 'n' roll.

Above: *The young Dick Clark.*
Right: *Clark at his desk while young 1950s dancers perform on* American Bandstand.
Left: *In* Cinderella *(1957), Julie Andrews was Cinderella and Jon Cypher was Prince Charming. In the box are Howard Lindsay and Dorothy Stickney.*

THE FIRST SCIENCE-FICTION ANTHOLOGY

One of the most imaginative script writers of the golden age of television drama in the mid-1950s was Rod Serling, creator of 'Patterns,' 'Requiem for a Heavyweight' and other memorable plays. In 1959 he became the host and chief scriptwriter for the memorable weekly program, *The Twilight Zone*, which ran from 2 October of that year until 5 September 1965.

The stories that Serling (with occasional contributions by scriptwriters Charles Beaumont, Richard Matheson and Earl Hamner, who was later to create *The Waltons*) wrote were unusual and offbeat, and often had ironic twists. A hypochondriac (David Wayne) makes an immortality pact with the devil, but tiring of life, he commits a murder, hoping to be executed – he gets a life sentence. An intellectual (Burgess Meredith) can't find time to read, but comes the time of a nuclear attack when he is the only survivor, he breaks his glasses.

As Serling would say at the beginning of every episode: 'There is a fifth dimension beyond that which is known to man. It is a dimension as vast as space and timeless as infinity. It is the middle ground between light and shadow, between science and superstition, and it lies between the pit of man's fears and the summit of his knowledge. It is an area we call *The Twilight Zone*.' And at the end of the show, he would intone, '. . . and you, have you ever been there?'

Above right: *Rod Serling was one of the several gifted playwrights who wrote television dramas in the early days of network telecasting. In 1959 he became the host of the cerebral thriller series,* The Twilight Zone, *writing many of the scripts himself. He later performed the same functions on* Night Gallery, *which began on NBC in 1970, running for three years.*

Right: *Cliff Robertson (center), played a night club ventriloquist in 'The Dummy; (4 May 1962) on* The Twilight Zone.

THE FIRST VIOLENT CRIME SHOW

The Untouchables ran on ABC from 15 October 1959 to 10 September 1963. It was set in Chicago in the 1930s and was based on the real-life exploits of Treasury Agent Eliot Ness and his squad of T-Men, nicknamed 'The Untouchables.' Robert Stack played Ness in this show, which was consistently the most violent program on the tube, featuring the chatter of machine-gun fire and the squeal of tires on the Chicago streets. The weekly bloodbath at times would feature three wild shootouts in a single hour. As *TV Guide* observed, 'In practically every episode a gang leader winds up stitched to a brick wall and full of bullets, or face down in a parking lot (and full of bullets), or hung up in an icebox, or run down in the street by a mug at the wheel of a big black Hudson touring car.'

The program was also in trouble on two other accounts. The United States Bureau of Prisons objected to the actions of prison officials, who were portrayed as less than professional, in the episodes involving Al Capone during his stay at the Alcatraz Penitentiary. And Italian-American civic groups complained that the criminals in the early seasons of the show were almost all of Italian descent, bearing obviously Italian names. The producers of *The Untouchables* took the latter complaint to heart, and by the end of the run, almost every ethnic group could lay claim to a villain who had appeared on the program. Even the Russians had not been ignored – one gangster was named Joe Vodka.

Left: *Robert Stack (right) played T-Man Eliot Ness, the hero of* The Untouchables. *One of his chief assistants was Rossi, played by Nicholas Georgiade.*

THE NIXON-KENNEDY DEBATES

The same Richard Nixon who had been saved by television in 1952 was undone by it in 1960. On 26 September 1960, the first of four hour-long televised debates between the presidential candidates, Richard M Nixon and John F Kennedy, was broadcast live from Chicago and carried on all three networks. This was made possible by a suspension of the 'equal time' section of the 1934 Communications Act, which was set up to give candidates from minority parties the same time on the air as Republican and Democratic candidates.

Veteran newsman Howard K Smith of CBS was the usual moderator, and the questioning panel included Robert Fleming of ABC, Stuart Novins of CBS, Charles Warren of Mutual Radio and Sander Vanocur of NBC. The questions were addressed to the candidates in turn, and the answers were limited to two and a half minutes. Each of the candidates was permitted a rebuttal of up to a minute and a half to his opponent's answer. The debate ended with a summary from each man.

This debate was an unprecedented event on television, and it may well have been the deciding factor in Kennedy's narrow victory over Nixon the following November. It wasn't so much what the men said, but rather their appearance that seemed to tip the scales. Kennedy looked youthful, urbane and in complete command of the situation. Nixon, on the other hand, was pale, tense, nervous, and in need of a shave. The American public chose the man who most inspired their confidence – John F Kennedy.

THE LAST HOWDY DOODY SHOW

Perhaps no children's television program ever acquired as many loyal fans as *Howdy Doody*, which premiered on 27 December 1947 and captured the first ever Peabody Award for the best children's program in 1948. Beginning with Buffalo Bob Smith's enthusuastic 'Say kids, what time is it?' and the resounding answer from the youngsters in the studio's 'Peanut Gallery' of 'It's Howdy Doody Time!!!' the show was a zany mélange of marionettes, gadgets and live performers playing a variety of outrageous roles.

Some of the supporting characters were Clarabell the Clown (originally played by Bob Keeshan, who went on to win fame as *Captain Kangaroo*), Chief Thunderthud of the Ooragnak (spell it backwards) Indians (Bill Le Cornec),

Princess Summerfall Winterspring (Judy Tyler) and Ugly Sam (Dayton Allen).

The 30 September 1960 show was the 2343rd episode of *Howdy Doody*, and Clarabell the Clown had never spoken a word on the show. On that fateful day, Clarabell (now played by Lew Anderson) darted about, carrying a sign bearing the word 'Surprise!' Howdy, Buffalo Bob and the other Doodyville characters spent most of the 30 minutes trying to learn what the surprise was but received only the honks of the clown's horn as an answer. The show was nearly at its close when Clarabell looked sadly into the camera, waved and spoke for the first time: 'Goodbye, kids.' NBC had cancelled them.

Above: *Bob Keeshan, who was later to become 'Captain Kangaroo,' was the first Clarabell the Clown on the* Howdy Doody *show.*
Right: *'Buffalo Bob' Smith with his celebrated marionette,* Howdy Doody.
Left: *One of the Kennedy (right) versus Nixon debates in October 1960. The moderator here is Frank McGee.*

THE FIRST COMMUNITY SING

Mitch Miller had been head of recording for Columbia Records, but he was no fan of rock 'n' roll. Consequently, he conceived the idea of packaging melodic and stylish music on 'Singalong' LPs – old favorites with the lyrics printed on the album cover. So successful was this venture that he ended up on television with this own show – *Sing Along With Mitch*. The program was introduced on *Ford Startime* in 1960 and had a limited run on NBC from 27 January 1961 to 21 April 1961, coming back from 28 September 1961 to 21 September 1964.

The show featured old favorites and some currently popular songs sung by Mitch's Sing Along Gang, the pre-teenage Sing Along Kids and by featured vocalists doing solos. These vocalists included three of Miller's discoveries – Leslie Uggams, Diana Trask and Sandy Stewart. When it came time for the audience to join in the singing, the lyrics would be flashed on the screen and the folks at home were invited to 'follow the bouncing ball.' Miller himself did very little except wave his baton at the orchestra and the viewers at home. The show also had lavish production numbers done by the James Starbuck Dancers.

For those three years the program was a sensation, and Mitch Miller had leaped from relative obscurity to national prominence. Indeed, when the *Sammy Davis Jr Show* on NBC began to falter in the spring of 1966, reruns were exhumed and Mitch Miller was on the air again.

Left: *A rehearsal of* Sing Along with Mitch. *Conductor Mitch Miller (center) with two of his* *bass players, Frank Carroll (right) and his 17-year-old son, Jim Carroll.*

THE FIRST AMERICAN IN SPACE

The eyes of America were glued to their television sets on 5 May 1961, when a Redstone rocket lifted a Mercury Capsule to a distance of 300 miles and a height of 113 miles above the surface of the Earth. The capsule carried the astronaut Alan B Shepard Jr, and it was the first time that an American had been sent into space. Traveling at a speed of 4375 miles per hour, Shepard and the *Freedom 7*, as the space capsule was named, were proving the possibility of space flight, and it was all being watched by the television cameras.

A mere 15 minutes and 22 seconds later, Shepard, inside the capsule, floated down into the ocean under an orange and white parachute. Then came the words from the astronaut, 'Everything is A-OK.' Those words were to become famous in headlines all over the world. America's first man in space had come through with flying colors. People around the world rejoiced and pinched themselves to make sure it really wasn't some far-fetched dream. The flight had been textbook perfect; indeed, it was what might have been called routine. But it added immeasurable to the National Aeronautics and Space Administration's confidence in the space program. Alan Shepard had survived his flight in fine style. There was an intensive two-day medical study in the Bahamas, but in the words of one of his doctors, 'He didn't even need a band aid.'

Right: *Astronaut Alan Shepard is taken aboard the rescue craft after his historic flight on 5 May 1961.*

Above: *Vice-President Lyndon Johnson (left), President John F Kennedy and First Lady Jacqueline Kennedy watching the Shepard space flight.*

THE FIRST AMERICAN IN SPACE ORBIT

The television cameras were on hand again on 20 February 1962 when the *Friendship 7*, with astronaut John Glenn Jr aboard, blasted off from Cape Canaveral, Florida. Four hours, 55 minutes and 23 seconds later, Glenn had finished his flight, having orbited the Earth three times – the first American in history to do that.

Sixteen orbital tracking stations existed around the Earth, and during the flight each one had maintained contact with the others by means of open telephones. Each kept a record of flight data as the capsule passed within range of the station. The electronic equipment required for these stations was nothing short of mind-boggling. There were clocks to synchronize timing to one five-thousandth of a second, computers that could calculate and plot the orbit of the capsule halfway around the world in seconds, and the most accurate radar in the world. Five foreign nations were involved in the tracking network: Australia, Mexico, Bermuda, Nigeria and Zanzibar.

The orbit, which swung from roughly 32 degrees north to 32 degrees south, was designed to keep the capsule traveling as much over water or US territory as possible. Each orbit, however, varied slightly because of the Earth's rotation. Three orbits only were planned because further trips would carry the astronaut outside the Atlantic splash-down area. But three were enough to make it a success.

Below: *Astronaut John Glenn in his space capsule during his flight on 20 February 1962.*

Right: *The Friendship 7 on its three-orbit flight around the Earth.*

THE CIVIL RIGHTS MARCH
ON WASHINGTON

The period of the early 1960s was a time of ferment among American blacks who were fighting for their civil rights. Led by Dr Martin Luther King Jr, they were involved in peaceful protests aimed at eradicating the 'Jim Crow' policies so often found in the United States, particularly in the South. Some of their actions brought violent reprisals from Southern whites, but the terrorism generated a huge groundswell of support for the civil rights movement, and led President John F Kennedy to push for the passage of a strong Civil Rights Act outlawing discrimination.

On 28 August 1963, The March on Washington, organized by civil rights leaders who wished to work peacefully for desegregation and equal opportunity for all Americans, took place. Some 250,000 people participated in this mass rally and heard Dr Martin Luther King Jr make his famous impassioned speech: 'I have a dream that one day the nation will rise up and live out the true meaning of its creed . . . all men are created equal.'

The television cameras were there to cover this important news event. One of the most penetrating comments on the rally was spoken by Frank Reynolds of NBC: 'There comes a time – there even comes a moment – in the affairs of men, when they sense that their lives are being altered forever – that an old order is dying and a new one is being born.'

THE FIRST EDUCATIONAL TELEVISION SUPERSTAR

The first major personality to appear on National Educational Television/Public Broadcasting System was not a puppet or a man in a buttoned-down sweater or a man with an English accent explaining dramatic shows – it was an irrepressible, sometimes giddy, sometime clumsy, very tall woman with a high-pitched voice. Not only that, she was not an entertainer but rather a cook. Cooking shows were nothing new to television. As far back as 1947, famed chef Dione Lucas was preparing food on the CBS show *To The Queen's Taste*. But this was different.

Julia Child, broadcasting from her studio kitchen at the WGBH/PBS studio in Boston, began her first program of cooking tips, *The French Chef*, in 1962, and captured the hearts of America. Millions watched her seemingly inept work (even though she might drop something from time to time, the gustatory delights came out unscathed) in preparing *cordon bleu* meals. The program ran until 1973. For a half hour every week huge audiences would tune in, because, while they might not be interested in French cooking, they wanted to see Julia.

She returned from 1978 to 1979 with another half-hour cooking show on PBS – *Julia Child & Company*, and later reappeared on *Dinner at Julia's*. Unlike her previous two shows, the latest program emphasized the cuisine of America.

Along the way, she picked up an Emmy from the National Academy of Television Arts and Sciences in 1966 and a George Foster Peabody Broadcasting Award in 1964 – both for *The French Chef*.

Above: *Some of the more than 200,000 persons who marched on Washington in August 1963, gathering at the Washington Monument and marching to the Lincoln Memorial.*

Opposite top: *The Reverend Dr Martin Luther King Jr addressing the crowds at the Washington march.*
Right: *Julia Child, the* French Chef, *attacking an onion.*

President John F Kennedy and First Lady Jacqueline Kennedy alight from Air Force One at Dallas Love Field, 22 November 1963.

KENNEDY IS ASSASSINATED

On 22 November 1963, President and Mrs John F Kennedy were in a motorcade riding from the airport to downtown Dallas while on a 'fence-mending' tour of Texas. Shots rang out and Kennedy slumped, mortally wounded. The president was pronounced dead at 1 PM (CST) and Lyndon Johnson was sworn in at 2:30 PM. Those were the bare bones of the tragic event.

As Johnson later said, 'Television's remarkable performance in communicating news of President John F Kennedy's assassination and the events that followed was a source of sober satisfaction to all Americans.' But oddly enough, it was a radio man who got the news to the nation first. Dan Rather, the Southwest Bureau chief for CBS news, was waiting for the motorcade when two limousines raced by him. Rather saw enough to send him rushing to the local CBS radio station, where he called the hospital and learned that the president was dead. Rather got the information on the radio 17 minutes before confirmation of the death was aired on television.

Walter Cronkite, the CBS anchor man in New York, was the first on the air with a television bulletin. At 1:30 (EST) he was in the studio when the news came in, and he was immediately put on camera to make the announcement, pre-empting the soap opera, *As the World Turns.* That began the epic four days of what was thought by many to be television's finest hour.

For four whole days, most people in the United States and many of those throughout the world sat glued to the television set as history took place before their eyes. Watching the sad return of Air Force One, bearing the new president, Lyndon Johnson, as well as the body of his predecessor, back to Andrews Air Force Base, outside Washington, and seeing for themselves the terrible stains on Jackie Kennedy's suit brought the disaster home.

On the rainy Saturday, as dignitaries began to arrive in Washington, and the President's coffin was brought to the East Room of the White House for a private family Mass, television reports for all over the world showed a world, not just a nation, in horror-struck disbelief and in universal mourning. In the afternoon of 22 November 1963, Dallas police had captured Lee Harvey Oswald in a movie theater where he had fled after shooting a policeman who had noticed his suspicious behavior. Oswald was a former expatriate to Russia who had returned to the United States. He was charged with having shot President John F Kennedy and Governor John Connally of Texas (who was riding in the limousine with the president) from the sixth-floor window of the Dallas Book Depository. On 24 November, the American public actually saw on their television screens a real murder. The alleged assassin was being removed from the Dallas Police Headquarters to a safer jail, when a local nightclub owner, Jack Ruby, walked up to the handcuffed Oswald and shot him dead.

It was NBC who had carried the story live. The network had just completed a report from Hyannisport, Massachusetts, when anchorman Frank McGee in New York heard correspondent Tom Pettit calling from the Dallas Police Station, 'Give me air! Give me air!' McGee immediately had the network switch to Dallas just as Oswald was being led to a car in the basement of the jail. Then Ruby

President John F Kennedy in the car after being shot.

President Lyndon Johnson is sworn in following the assassination.

Jack Ruby (with back to camera) advances on Oswald.

came onto the scene, a shot was heard, and Oswald gasped, grabbed his side and fell to the ground. The audience and the newscasters were equally stunned. CBS's Charles Collingwood said, 'Violence had not yet subdued its appetite.' ABC's Howard K Smith lamented, 'We will never hear this man's story.'

Back in Washington, on Sunday, the ritual and ceremony of the state funeral began with the transfer of the President's coffin by horse-drawn caisson to the Rotunda of the Capitol where it would lie in state until the funeral the following day. Again, the television cameras brought the watching public pictures that would be indelibly etched in their minds. The two small Kennedy children in their pale blue coats. The skittish, riderless horse following the fallen leader in a ritual older than Christianity. The unforgettable silence broken only by the clatter of hooves on pavement and the sound of muffled drums. The eulogies by members of the Senate and the House were carried by all three networks. Evening memorial concerts were interrupted for the arrival of more heads of state and the cameras also watched the thousands, waiting throughout the night to pay their respects, moving quietly past the flag-draped coffin.

Monday, 25 November 1963, had been declared a national Day of Mourning by the new president Lyndon Johnson, and again the world watched as the procession moved from the White House to the Capitol, and then to the Roman Catholic Church of St Matthews for the Low Pontifical Mass offered by Cardinal Cushing of Boston, and eventually to Arlington National Cemetary for the burial and the lighting of the Eternal Flame. The funeral was over, but television had discovered depths it had not known it possessed. The medium had proved that it was truly a window on the world that could capture deep human emotion.

Above: *The caisson bearing President John F Kennedy's coffin procedes toward Arlington National Cemetery.*
Left: *The widow, Jacqueline Kennedy, walked in the funeral procession, flanked by the fallen president's brothers, Bobby (left) and Ted.*
Far left top: *President Kennedy's casket enters the White House. Mrs Kennedy follows it.*
Far left below: *The casket of the President is loaded onto the caisson as the family looks on.*
Below: *The casket of the president being carried to the grave in Arlington National Cemetery.*

THE FIRST SATIRE PROGRAM

THE BEATLES ARRIVE

Ed Sullivan had been a mainstay on Sunday night on the Columbia Broadcasting System since 1948 with his variety show that featured everything from operatic sopranos, rock stars and chorus lines to comedians, ballet companies and scenes from Broadway plays. All this glitter, plus his lack of stage presence (his voice, mispronunciations and stiff

Among the tributes that flooded into the United States after the assassination of President Kennedy was the extraordinary effort by the cast of the British satire, *That Was The Week That Was*. The program, which had been put together in just 16 hours, was shown twice that weekend, once on Sunday night, and again on Monday evening. Indeed, the entire script was read into the Congressional Record in recognition of outpouring of emotion inspired by Kennedy's assassination.

An American version of the program, known commonly as *TW3* ran on NBC from 10 January 1964 to 4 May 1965, and by the end of the run everyone was exhausted. The setting and atmosphere resembled that of a cabaret, and it was done live, so it became a highly topical and up-to-the-minute show.

The purpose was to poke fun at people in high places, and the program used comedy sketches, blackouts, musical production numbers and 'news' reports. The hosts were Eliot Reid in the first season and David Frost in the second. The sketches were sometimes brutal – a Catholic tells his Jewish friend that the Pope had exonerated Jews from the responsibility for Jesus's death, but the Jew still couldn't join his country club. News reports were mind-boggling – UN paratroopers being dropped by Guatemalan Air Force planes on Jackson, Mississippi to rescue civil rights workers.

Singer-writer-composer-pianist-mathematics instructor Tom Lehrer contributed some of his most vitriolic melodies – 'The Vatican Rag,' 'Smut,' 'The Folk Song Army,' 'National Brotherhood Week,' 'Pollution' and 'What Ever Became of Hubert?' among them.

The American cast included Nancy Ames ('The TW3 Girl'), Henry Morgan, Phyllis Newman, Buck Henry, Bob Dishy, Doro Merande, Alan Alda, Tom Bosley and Burr Tillstrom's puppets.

mannerisms were widely imitated by professional impressionists), made *The Ed Sullivan Show* a 24-year wonder. Sullivan really knew how to ferret out talent and put on a good show.

One of his all-time top rated shows was broadcast on 9 February 1964, when the Beatles made their premiere American appearance and brought down the house. These four Liverpudlians – Ringo Starr, George Harrison, John Lennon and Paul McCartney – were flown over by Sullivan from England to appear on his show. Already pop music idols in England, the Beatles had gathered a huge following in the United States, since their earliest record albums had

preceeded them.

The result was a sensation. All over the country young female (and some male) rock 'n' roll fans were fainting on their living room floors, while their parents were fuming about the barbaric music the four lads were creating, obviously forgetting how they themselves tortured their own parents with boogie-woogie records. Later both the Beatles and the parents mellowed, and that particular generation gap disappeared.

Far left: *David Frost and Nancy Ames of* TW3.

Below: *Ed Sullivan with The Beatles – 9 February 1964.*

THE FIRST EVENING SOAP OPERA

The first prime time soap opera to become a success was *Peyton Place*, based on Grace Metalious's enormously popular and steamy novel about the sexual goings-on in the lives of the residents of Peyton Place, a small New England town. The program ran from 15 September 1964 to 2 June 1969, and in the first season it was telecast twice a week and both segments cracked Nielsen's top twenty that year. In the 1964-1965 season, the show was pushed up to three times a week. During the final seasons it went back to twice a week.

There was a huge cast whose members drifted in and out of the story line over the run of the show, but, at least in the beginning, at the center of most of the drama was bookshop proprietor Constance Mackenzie (Dorothy Malone), whose own dark secret was the mysterious circumstances surrounding the birth of her daughter Allison (Mia Farrow). Among the other members of the cast were old television hands and new talent just waiting to be discovered. Some of them were: Ed Nelson (Dr Michael Rossi), Warner Ander-

son (Matthew Swain), Ryan O'Neal (Rodney Harrington), Kent Smith (Dr Robert Morton), Erin O'Brien Moore (Nurse Choate) and Mariette Hartley (Dr Claire Morton). Leslie Nielsen (Dr Vincent Markham), Lee Grant (Stella Chernak), Barbara Parkins (Betty Anderson), John Kerr (District Attorney John Fowler), George Macready (Martin Peyton) were also in the cast. Macready was replaced by Wilfred Hyde-White temporarily in 1967.

The plot, like most soaps, was pretty complicated. Constance was able to marry Allison's real father, Elliott Carson, when he got out of prison. Allison married Rodney, but when Mia Farrow decided to leave the series, Allison 'disappeared.' Harrington was tried for murder. Steven Cord (James Douglas) and Dr Rossi found themselves involved in sexual hanky-panky, and Rossi, like Harrington, was tried for murder. Martin Peyton, the town's patriarch, was wooed by a young woman in order to get his money, but he conveniently died. The continuing stories were varied, but the main themes were sex and violence.

THE FIRST 'PEANUTS' SPECIAL

The comic strip 'Peanuts,' drawn by Charles M Schulz, had delighted children and adults since 1950, and appeared in some 2000 newspapers around the world. So it seemed natural to make a television special out of the charming strip that features Charlie Brown, the constant loser; busybody Lucy Van Pelt and her nervous brother Linus; Snoopy the wonder dog and Schroeder, the fan of Beethoven.

The first of more than a score of 'Peanuts' specials appeared on CBS on 9 December 1965 and was called *A Charlie Brown Christmas*. The program won both an Emmy and a George Foster Peabody Award. The first showing of the program (it is regularly rerun during the Christmas season) drew more than 50 percent of the viewing audience in the United States.

The voices used in the 'Peanuts' specials are those of young children, and new boys and girls are auditioned every two years, since as the small actors grow, their voices change and become too mature. The exception to this rule is the voice of Snoopy, which is always done by Bill Melendez, the co-producer of the specials.

From this humble beginning came such other television triumphs as *It's the Great Pumpkin, Charlie Brown* and *Be My Valentine, Charlie Brown*, but the original is still the best.

Above: A Charlie Brown Christmas.
Far left: *Barbara Parkins in* Peyton Place.
Below: *Bill Cosby (left) and Robert Culp in* I Spy.

THE FIRST ADVENTURE PROGRAM TO STAR A BLACK ACTOR

I Spy, which ran on NBC from 15 September 1965 to 2 September 1968, followed the adventures of two American undercover agents who traveled around the world on various assignments disguised as a professional tennis player and his trainer. The program was witty, adventurous and well-done, and it was the first noncomedy show to star a black actor – Bill Cosby.

Cosby played Alexander 'Scotty' Scott, a Temple University graduate and a Rhodes Scholar – a spy who posed as the trainer of Kelly Robinson (played by Robert Culp), a Princeton-educated secret agent, who masqueraded as a tennis pro. The program had its share of cloak-and-dagger action, but it never took itself too seriously, and there was a great deal of irony and subtle humor in the dialogue.

Scott was the one who spoke several languages and provided much of the humor, and Cosby proved that he was not only a great comedian (which everyone knew anyway), but also that he was an accomplished serious actor. Robinson was an authority on law and Culp proved that he was also a most competent performer. Together, the two men were convincing, and audiences knew that they were two good friends who trusted and respected each other. The two were obviously dedicated to their country and their profession, but they often questioned the motives and purposes behind some of the jobs they had to do.

JUDY'S FINEST HOUR

Some of the greatest of all of America's stars and popular personalities just couldn't seem to make a transition to television successfully. Two examples from radio were Ed Wynn and the acerbic Fred Allen. Singers who were enormously gifted, compelling in person and on records, also tried and failed at regular television shows. Frank Sinatra and Judy Garland are two prime examples.

The Columbia Broadcasting System had high hopes for *The Judy Garland Show*, which ran from 19 September 1963 to 29 March 1964, but they never materialized, perhaps because it was running opposite the phenomenally successful *Bonanza* (the number-one rated show that year) on NBC. The show featured big glossy production numbers. Guest stars were everywhere – Mel Tormé, Ethel Merman, Danny Kaye and Mickey Rooney. But nothing seemed to work. The format was changed to be more folksy, with Judy chatting with guest stars and singing a little, but this didn't work, either. Then several of the shows during the last two months were simple ones – a plain set with Judy and her guests just singing. That was the best format, but it was too late.

There was one magical moment during the run, however. In 1964 she had two sensational young guests: her 18-year-old daughter, Liza Minnelli, and another unknown, 22-year-old Barbra Streisand. All that the three of them did was sing – solos, duets and trios, but the audience knew it was truly a magical moment.

The 18-year-old Liza Minnelli sings with her mother on The Judy Garland Show. *Her sister Lorna Luft joined them later.*

THE FIRST CAMP SHOW

Batman was the first television show that deliberately camped it up, playing its adventure stories for laughs. This was fair, of course, since it was based on the comic strip of the same name that was created by cartoonist Bob Kane. The show ran on ABC from 12 January 1966 to 14 March 1968, appearing twice a week – both half-hour shows were in the top ten during the first year of broadcasting.

It was never taken seriously, even by the people who appeared in it, and guest star villains had field days hamming it up and chewing the scenery. The fight scenes were punctuated by animated 'Pows,' 'Bops,' 'Bangs' and 'Thuds' that flashed on the screen when a blow was struck.

The structure was simple. Bruce Wayne (Adam West) was a millionaire who fought crime wearing the costume of Batman. His ward, Dick Grayson (Burt Ward) joined him as Robin the Boy Wonder. The only one who knew their secret identities was their loyal butler, Alfred Pennyworth (Alan Napier). The Caped Crusader and the Boy Wonder, together known as the Dynamic Duo, worked out of an underground Batlab, using their Batmobile, talking on the Batphone or watching for the Batsignal.

Many entertainment personalities were delighted to appear on the show as guest villains. Among the more memorable were Burgess Meredith (The Penguin), Cesar Romero (The Joker), Vincent Price (Egghead) and Milton Berle (Louie the Lilac).

Above: *Bruce Wayne, played by Adam West, gets a call on the red Batphone as Dick Grayson, played by Burt Ward, looks on.*

Right: *Wayne still talks on the Batphone as Grayson looks on, but this time they are garbed as Batman and Robin.*

Following spread: *Shelley Winters was a villainess on a* Batman *episode, who caught the Dynamic Duo.*

THE FIRST SERIOUS FUTURISTIC PROGRAM

Star Trek, which ran on NBC from 8 September 1966 to 2 September 1969, unlike such previous science-fiction shows such as *Captain Video*, was a serious and well-done program. Set some 200 years in the future, it told of the adventures of the starship USS *Enterprise*, a cruiser-sized spacecraft whose mission was to 'seek out new life and new civilizations' in outer space as directed by the United Federation of Planets.

The *Enterprise* had a crew of 400, but there were only eight principals in the cast: Captain James Kirk (William Shatner); Science Officer Spock (Leonard Nimoy), an intelligent unemotional man who was the son of a Vulcan father and an Earthling mother; Dr Leonard 'Bones' McCoy (DeForest Kelley), the ship's medical officer; Montgomery 'Scotty' Scott (James Doohan), the chief engineer; Lieutenant Uhura (Nichelle Nichols), the communications officer; Mr Sulu (George Takei), a navigator; Christine Chapel (Majel Barrett), the chief nurse; and Ensign Chekov (Walter Koenig), another navigator.

The odd thing about the program was that it became more popular in reruns than it was when it was originally broadcast. It attracted a fiercely loyal cult following (fans were called 'Trekkies') and this group was most assuredly the reason that NBC renewed the show for its third season after planning to scrap it. Indeed, when the show was finally dropped in 1969, the network received more than one million protest letters.

Only 78 episodes of *Star Trek* were produced, but the program certainly had a great afterlife. From 1973 to 1975 NBC modified the plots and ran a Saturday morning cartoon *Star Trek*, with the voices being dubbed by members of the original cast. Then, in 1979, a motion picture version, reuniting most of the original cast, appeared – the first of a series of *Star Trek* films – one of the few times that a television program spun off a movie.

Left: *The crew of the* Enterprise *in unusual spacesuits.*

Above: *Captain Kirk and his crew on the bridge.*

THE FIRST PSYCHEDELIC TELEVISION PROGRAM

Rowan & Martin's Laugh-In, which ran on NBC from 22 January 1968 to 14 May 1973, was more a television 'happening' than a comedy show. This innovative program would feature fast-paced blackouts, sketches, one-liners and cameo appearances by celebrities (even Richard Nixon was seen repeating one of the show's gag lines, 'Sock it to me'). *Laugh-In* was a combination of Olsen and Johnson's *Helzapoppin'*, the madcap antics of the Keystone Kops and the topical satire of *That Was The Week That Was*.

The regular cast was wonderful, and some of the people who came to prominence on the show were Goldie Hawn, Lily Tomlin, Ruth Buzzi, Judy Carne, Eileen Brennen, Arte Johnson, Henry Gibson, Jo Anne Worley, Alan Sues and Richard Dawson. The program contributed several catch phrases to the American idiom: 'Sock it to me,' 'Ring my

Far left: *Dan Rowan (left) and Dick Martin listen to comic Arte Johnson tell a horrible joke from the joke wall, while Goldie Hawn looks on from above.*

Above: *Put upon Dan Rowan (left) tries to explain something to the ever-dense Dick Martin in a comedy exchange on* Rowan & Martin's Laugh-In.

chimes,' 'Look that up in your Funk & Wagnall's,' 'Verrry interesting,' 'Beautiful downtown Burbank,' 'Here come de judge' and 'You bet your bippy.'

Some of the features of the show were The Cocktail Party and its inane conversations, Letters to *Laugh-In*, The Flying Fickle Finger of Fate Award, *Laugh-In* Looks at the News (of the past, present and future), Hollywood News with Ruth Buzzi, gags written on the undulating body of a girl in a bikini, and the joke wall, in which cast members popped out of windows to throw away one-liners.

TELEVISION AND THE VIETNAM WAR

From the first landing of American troops in Vietnam, US involvement had come under strong criticism at home. Although President Lyndon B Johnson was able to maintain the support of most Americans by repeatedly assuring them that the enemy was being steadily defeated, the huge Communist offensive in January 1968 burst the bubble.

Television seemed to be participating in the war rather than merely documenting it. In covering the fighting, every night it seemed to present footage of battles and carnage, and this coverage was regarded as the sufficient motivater in changing American's attitudes toward the war. The way it was reported, the selection of material, and the bias of reporters and anchormen recast American opinion. Corres-

pondents grew open, on the air and in public statement, about their opposition to the war.

As early as 1965 Walter Cronkite of CBS, after visiting South Vietnam, reported disillusionment with the American aims in Vietnam. At the time there were polls that indicated that Cronkite was the most trusted person in the United States. He was a father figure to millions of Americans, and his condemnation of the war was probably the most important factor in turning the country against the hostilities and it resulted in Johnson's announcement of 31 March 1968 of both the cessation of bombing north of the 21st parallel in Vietnam and his own decision not to seek re-election.

Above: *Marines of D Company, 1st Battalion, Fifth Marines, in the streets of Hué on the north side of the Perfumed River during the Vietnam War.*
Left: *A monitor boat from the River Assault Flotilla One uses flamethrowers to destroy possible enemy ambush sites, along a narrow stream in the Mekong Delta.*
Right above: *Utility helicopters flying a mission during the Vietnam War.*
Right below *Searching for North Vietnamese snipers in the thickets of bamboo.*

Left: *Flight deck crewmen carry on their duties on the nuclear-powered attack aircraft carrier*

USS Enterprise. *These aircraft provided cover and support during the Saigon evacuation.*

Above: *A member of Company A destroys a hut with a flame thrower.*

Top: *In Operation 'White-Wing,' helicopters moved personnel into an assault area.*

KING IS ASSASSINATED

The man who moved the consciousness of the nation – the man who in one year (1964) received an honorary doctorate from Yale University, the Kennedy Peace Prize and the Nobel Peace Prize – Dr Martin Luther King Jr – was assassinated on 4 April 1968. The killer was a sniper who shot King as he stood on his motel room balcony in Memphis, Tennessee, and immediately television began its massive coverage of the story. King had been on a civil rights mission to Tennessee.

Fear and violence mounted as the shock of the assassination spread across the nation and set off a wave of black rioting and looting. Riots erupted in 63 cities as the black community expressed its outrage and grief. More than 150,000 mourners attended his funeral at his old Ebenezer Baptist Church in Atlanta, Georgia. And television cameras were following all of this. Indeed, the intense coverage did not relax until, on 8 June 1968, James Earl Ray, the assassin, was arrested in London and 24 June 1968, when a poor people's march on Washington that had been planned by the late Dr King had ended. In this march, which had begun on 2 May, caravans from all over the nation converged on the capital and set up camp on a 16-acre site named Resurrection City. Led by Ralph Abernathy, it included Southern blacks, Indians, Mexican-Americans and Appalachian whites, and was a fitting tribute to this great man.

Left: *The Reverend Martin Luther King Jr, who won the Nobel Prize for Peace in 1964, was fatally shot in Memphis, Tennessee in 1968.*

Below: *Coretta King (third from right), the widow of Dr Martin Luther King and the family mourn at the martyr's coffin.*

DEMOCRATIC
NATIONAL

THE 1968 DEMOCRATIC CONVENTION

On 26 August 1968 the Democratic National Convention convened in Chicago, and on 28 August, Hubert H Humphrey received the nomination as the party's presidential candidate. But more important than that, the convention was being held in the midst of police action against antiwar demonstrations by 'Yippies' outside the convention hall. The public's memories of the confrontations that they saw on television may have cost Humphrey victory in the presidential election.

There is little doubt that television was playing into the hands of the demonstrators who seemed to stage riots whenever they saw a TV camera. Many of the rioters were injured by the police actions, but many of the police were injured, too. One reporter pointed out that the Yippies had bought oven cleaner to spray at the police. At the end of the convention, Americans were divided about what they thought had happened. Some thought that it had been great theater. But others thought that the television coverage of the convention and the disturbances outside had become a national issue, with charges of distortions and unfair emphasis on police brutality.

Inside the hall, security was also beefed up. One moment that broke the tension occurred when NBC newsman John

Top: *Mrs Hubert H Humphrey (center) stands in front of her husband at the Chicago convention (1968).*

Above: *Delegates to the 1968 Chicago convention of the Democratic Party.*

Chancellor was arrested on the floor and said, 'This is John Chancellor, somewhere in custody.'

THE FIRST TELEVISION NEWSMAGAZINE

In its way, *60 Minutes* does resemble *Time* and *Newsweek*, with its opening table of contents, its feature news stories, its letters to the editor and its back of the book editorial opinions. The program began on CBS on 24 September 1968 and has been running ever since, along the way becoming the highest rated public affairs show in history, finishing in the Nielson Top Twenty Programs every year since 1977, and actually finishing Number One in 1980 and 1983.

This documentary series has always had a remarkable scope, delving into such stories as ITT lobbyist Dita Beard, Howard Hughes' supposed biographer Clifford Irving, Colonel Anthony Herbert's contention that Vietnamese war atrocities had been covered up, interviews with several principals in the Watergate coverup, drug dealing on an international scale, crime, dangerous working environments and the right to die. Many of the programs have led to social reform or the righting of wrongs.

The correspondents on the show have been Mike Wallace (in at the beginning), Harry Reasoner (1968-1970, left for ABC, then returned to the program in 1978), Morley Safer (1970 to the present), Dan Rather (1975-1981, when he left to become the replacement for Walter Cronkite as host of the *CBS Evening News*), Ed Bradley (1981 to the

September 1968
December 1970

Above: *The two original co-hosts of* 60 Minutes *from September 1968 until December 1970 – Harry Reasoner (left) and Mike Wallace.*

Below: *The* 60 Minutes *team has expanded to include Ed Bradley (top left), Morley Safer and Diane Sawyer.*

present) and Diane Sawyer (1984 to the present). Editorial opinions have been always a feature, these days being expressed by Andy Rooney.

THE FIRST MOON WALK

The television cameras were ready at the Kennedy Space Center on 16 July 1969 as astronauts Neil A Armstrong, Edwin E (Buzz) Aldrin Jr and Michael Collins blasted off in their Apollo-Saturn 11 mission to land on the moon. People all over the country watched this historic liftoff and they would later be treated to television pictures of the moon's surface and the first man to walk on that bleak satellite.

Everything went like clockwork. On July 20 1969, Apollo 11 achieved one of the greatest victories in the history of exploration. Nearly one-quarter of the world's population watched as the grayish figure of Neil Armstrong appeared, clambered down the ladder of the lunar module, and stepped on the surface of the moon in the Sea of Tranquility. As he stepped from the ladder, he remarked, 'That's one

Above: *Astronaut Neil A Armstrong descends the ladder to become the first man on the moon.*

Following spread: *Neil A Armstrong salutes the American flag that he has planted on the moon's surface.*

small step for a man, one giant leap for mankind.' Then he moved carefully through the moon's black shadows and blinding sunlight.

The three men returned to Earth on 24 July, but they had left some commemorative items on the moon. There was a small plaque which read, 'Here men from the planet Earth first set foot upon the moon, July, 1969 AD. We came in peace for all mankind.' Shoulder patches and medals were also left on the moon, as well as a silicon disk which had been etched with messages from the leaders of 73 countries.

THE FIRST IMPORTED MINISERIES

Left: *The Forsyte clan during the Victorian Era included (back row left) Lana Morris as Helene, Kenneth More as Young Jolyon, Joseph O'Connor as Old Jolyon, Margaret Tyzack as Winifred, (front center) Nyree Dawn Porter as Irene and Eric Porter as Soames.*

Right : *A scene from the 'A Family Wedding' episode from The Forsyte Saga, the BBC series shown in Britain in 1967 and two years later in the United States. Left to right: Eric Porter as Soames Forsyte, Cyril Luckam as Sir Lawrence Mont, Susan Hampshire as Fleur Forsyte and Nicholas Pennell as Michael Mont.*

One of the most startling success stories in television history occurred from 5 October 1969 to 29 March 1970, when millions of Americans gathered around their sets to watch, of all things, a miniseries imported from England. *The Forsyte Saga* had been produced in black and white in England, and it was a 26-part adaptation of English novelist John Galsworthy's series of books. Spanning the years from 1879 to 1926, it told of the lives of the members of a moderately wealthy English family against a backdrop of Victorian and Edwardian life up to the 1920s. And Americans became quite fascinated.

The fine cast included Kenneth More (as Jolyon 'Jo' Forsyte, the painter), Eric Porter (lawyer Soames Forsyte), Nyree Dawn Porter (Irene, first Soames' and later Jo's wife), Susan Hampshire (Soames' daughter Fleur), Margaret Tyzack (Winifred), Nicholas Pennell (Michael Mont), Joseph O'Connor (Jolyon 'Old Jolyon' Forsyte Sr), Fay Compton (Aunt Ann), Lana Morris (Helene), Martin Jarvis (Jon Forsyte), Ursula Howells (Frances) and George Woodbridge (Swithin).

Despite the fact that the characters spoke with English accents, despite the fact that the time frame was a less-than-thrilling period in English history, despite the fact that the program was in black and white, despite the fact that there was little action, National Educational Television had a hit on their hands. Due in part to the success of *The Forsyte Saga*, PBS was encouraged to begin the *Masterpiece Theatre* series.

AGNEW CRITICIZES TELEVISION

It was clear during the Nixon administration that the president was antagonistic toward the television medium. It was because of this opposition that Pat Buchanan, a speech writer, crafted a speech for Vice President Spiro T Agnew, which was presented in Des Moines, Iowa on 13 November 1969. All three networks covered the negative comments.

Agnew attacked 'a small group of men, numbering perhaps no more than a dozen anchormen, commentators and executive producers [who] settle upon the twenty minutes or so of film and commentary that's to reach the public . . . a tiny, enclosed fraternity of privileged men elected by no one and enjoying a monopoly sanction and licensed by government.'

Public opinion was split. There was no doubt that the speech was a political one that sought support for letting the administration say whatever it wanted to without criticism by the television people. But there was a grain of truth to it – the newsmen and producers on the networks had, on occasion, been guilty of distorting the truth. As one writer said about the television coverage of the 1968 Democratic National Convention, 'There was no way to challenge Walter Cronkite's catchphrase ['That's the way it is'] that so irritated disaffected viewers and say to him, "No, that isn't the way it is, at least not all of it."'

Below: *The then Vice-President Spiro T Agnew attacks the press.*

THE MOST SUCCESSFUL CHILDREN'S PROGRAM

Without doubt, *Sesame Street* is the most popular kids' show of all time, and perhaps the most educational one, to boot. It began its run on National Educational Television/PBS on 10 November 1969, and has been blending skits, songs, puppetry and animation to teach letters, numbers and grammatical concepts ever since. The program, the brainchild of Joan Ganz Cooney of the Children's Television Workshop, is set along a city street because it was designed primarily to appeal to inner-city preschoolers, but it appeals to children of all backgrounds.

Sesame Street's human performers have included Loretta Long (Susan), Matt Robinson and Roscoe Orman (Gordon), Bob McGrath (Bob), Will Lee (Mr Hooper), Northern J Calloway (David), Emilio Delgado (Luis) and Sonia Manzano (Maria). But perhaps the real stars are Jim Henson's Muppets – Ernie, Bert, Oscar the Grouch, the Cookie Monster and Big Bird. The latter is not exactly a puppet, but rather a life-size figure played first by Frank Oz and later by Carroll Spinney.

Music is important to the show, and many songs have been written for the series by Jeff Moss and Joe Raposo. Most of the shows are 'sponsored' by particular letters or numbers, which are presented as 'commercials.' Of course, this being PBS, there are no real sponsors.

Left: Sesame Street *cleverly combines Jim Henson's muppets with real people and children, including Maria (Sonia Manzano), Susan (Loretta Long), Gordon (Roscoe Orman) and Bob (Bob McGrath).*
Top right: *Oscar the Grouch lives in a garbage can on Sesame Street.*
Right: *Big Bird (created by Jim Henson and played by Carroll Spinney) is one of the stars of Sesame Street – that wonderful Public Broadcasting System program that has taught so many children to love learning by making it fun.*

MASTERPIECE THEATRE

The miniseries that began the classic *Masterpiece Theatre* series on PBS – the long-running series so ably and eruditely hosted by Alistair Cooke – was *The First Churchills*. It ran weekly from 10 January to 28 March 1971, was produced by the British Broadcasting Company and starred Susan Hampshire, John Neville, John Standing and James Villiers as Charles II.

The story focused on the religious, political and military turbulence in late seventeenth century and early eighteenth century England and told the story of John Churchill, the founder of the dynasty that was to produce the great statesman, Winston Spencer Churchill. He began as a soldier of fortune, married Sarah Jennings, a lady in waiting to the daughter of the Duke of York, became the hero of the Battle of Blenheim and ended as a failed enemy of the Tories.

Masterpiece Theatre is undoubtedly the finest continuous program of television drama in America's history of the medium. The series have been of varying lengths and have covered all sorts of matters, from historical costume-pieces to light detective fare, and have come from both commercial and non-commercial television studios (mostly British). Through the years the productions – the masterpieces – have included *Elizabeth R* (with Glenda Jackson); *Murder Must Advertise* (with Ian Carmichael as Lord Peter Wimsey) and *Disraeli* (with Ian McShane). Many of them actually were based on literary masterpieces: *I, Claudius* (with Derek Jacobi); *How Green Was My Valley* and *Cousin Bette*.

One *Masterpiece Theatre* series ran for 52 episodes over four seasons – 6 January to 31 March 1974, 3 November 1974 to 26 January 1975, 4 January to 28 March 1976, and 16 January to 1 May 1977. Unlike most of the miniseries on the program, *Upstairs, Downstairs* was not borrowed from the movies, from the theater, or from a work of fiction. It merely told the story of an upper- or upper-middle-class family in London and their lives from 1903 to 1930, following the Richard Bellamys of Eaton Place (and their

servants) from the imperial days of Edward VII's reign through World War I and the social changes of the 1920s. Ten earlier episodes, covering the late 1890s, were never shown on American televison.

Featured in the cast upstairs were: David Langton as Richard Bellamy, the head of the family and member of Parliament; Rachel Gurney as Lady Marjorie Bellamy, his wife who went down on the *Titanic*; Simon Williams as their son James; Meg Wynn Owen as Hazel, James's wife; and Leslie-Ann Down as Georgina Worsley, Richard Bellamy's ward. Appearing in the downstairs household were: Gordon Jackson as Hudson, the faithful and proper butler; Jean Marsh as Rose, the parlour maid (she and Eileen Atkins had been the ones to suggest the original idea for the series); Angela Baddeley as Mrs Bridges, the cook; Christopher Beeny as Edward, the footman and later chauffeur; Jenny Tomasin as Ruby, the scullery maid; and Jacqueline Tong as Daisy, the upstairs maid.

Above: *Susan Hampshire and John Neville as Sarah and John Churchill, on their wedding* *night in* The First Churchills – *the first* Masterpiece Theatre *shown in the US.*

Left: *In* Cousin Bette, *another* Masterpiece Theatre *offering, Bette (Margaret Tyzack), in order to punish the family that has treated her like a poor relation, lures one of its members, Crevel (John Brayans) into an affair with another woman.*
Below: *The triumphant wedding of the Marquis of Stockbridge (Anthony Andrews) to Georgina Worsley (Leslie-Ann Down). Toasting them, left to right, are the parlor maid Rose (Jean Marsh), the cook Mrs Bridges (Angela Baddeley), the scullery maid Ruby (Jenny Tomasin), the butler Hudson (Gordon Jackson), the upstairs maid Daisy (Jacqueline Tong) and the chauffeur Edward (Christopher Beeny). This was the final episode of* Upstairs, Downstairs.

THE FIRST INFLUENTIAL SITUATION COMEDY

All in the Family premiered on 12 January 1971 on CBS and continued until 21 September 1983 (the title was changed to *Archie Bunker's Place* at the end of the 1978 season). The show was the first situation comedy to deal openly with bigotry, prejudice and politics. Previously forbidden topics such as abortion, birth control, mate-swapping, menopause and homosexuality were handled successfully, and taboo words, such as 'spic,' 'hebe' and 'spade' appeared in the scripts.

Originally, there were four characters who made the show what it was – the number one program in the nation for its first five years – Carroll O'Connor (as Archie Bunker), Jean Stapleton (as Edith 'Dingbat' Bunker, his wife), Rob Reiner (as Mike 'Meathead' Stivic) and Sally Struthers (as Gloria Bunker Stivic). Archie was a working class person who hated everyone who was not white, Protestant and Anglo-Saxon. His biggest problem, however, was that he seemed to be unable to escape the people he was prejudiced against. He had to work with a racially-mixed group of people. A black family, the Jeffersons, lived next door. His son-in-law was a Polish-American. He eventually had to take in a Puerto Rican boarder. Of course, Archie always lost his arguments, but the program held up a mirror to the audience and made them look at it.

Below: *The stars of* All in the Family – *Jean Stapleton (Edith Bunker), Carroll O'Connor (Archie Bunker), Sally Struthers* (Gloria Stivic) and Rob Reiner (Mike Stivic).
Right: *The family with baby Joey.*

THE OLYMPIC TRAGEDY

Jim McKay had been the host of ABC's *Wide World of Sports*, telling of the thrill of victory and the agony of defeat, since its inception on 29 April 1961. So it seemed only natural when ABC was awarded the contract to telecast the 1972 Summer Olympic Games from Munich, West Germany, that he would be the anchor man for the programs.

On 5 September 1972, eight members of the Arab Black September terrorist group invaded the Israeli dormitory at the Olympic Village and killed two members of the Israeli squad. After tense negotiations that lasted 23 hours, the terrorists and nine hostages were flown to an airport where five terrorists and all the hostages were killed in a gun battle.

Suddenly McKay was forced to revert to his old newsman days, announcing the events as they happened, hypothesizing what might happen next, even whipping the rest of his sports team of broadcasters into shape and making them, for a time, real newsmen, too. The sportscenter studio became a newsroom and McKay was on camera for hours. His solid handling of the reporting of the events constituted the only first hand information that was available to the American public, and McKay was masterful in combining hardline news with empathy, sympathy and concern. For his splendid work that day he was awarded an Emmy for Outstanding Achievement in Coverage of Special Events.

Above: *Jim McKay of ABC.*
Top: *An Arab stands guard at* the Israeli dormitory during the terrorist invasion.

THE WATERGATE HEARINGS

On 17 June 1972, Washington police arrested five men for breaking into the Democratic National Headquarters in the Watergate Complex. All five were employed by the Committee to Reelect the President and were trying to obtain political material from the opposing party. Later two White House aides, G Gordon Liddy and E Howard Hunt, were arrested and tied to the break-in. The Watergate cauldron began to boil, and on 7 February 1973 the Senate established a Select Committee on Presidential Campaign Activities to investigate the conspiracy. The chairman of the committee was Senator Sam Ervin of North Carolina. The public hearings, which were televised, began on 17 May 1973.

By the time that the hearings began, many highups in the Nixon administration had resigned, but the president still denied knowledge of the whole affair. On 25 June, John Dean, a former presidential counsel, told the committee that Nixon was involved in a Watergate coverup and on 16 July it was revealed that Nixon had had tapes made of his conversations in the Oval Office. All America was shocked.

The Senate panel subpoenaed the tapes, but Nixon rejected the subpoena. Ervin, however, was adamant, saying 'The best evidence of what these tapes say is the tapes themselves.' By the time the evidence was all in, Nixon had resigned and had been saved from impeachment by new President Gerald Ford. And thanks to television the public had seen it all.

Above: *The house Judiciary Committee begins hearings on the Nixon impeachment over the Watergate scandal.*
Right: *President Richard Nixon making his television speech concerning Watergate.*
Left: *The Watergate Hearings became popular television fare. The questioners here are Senator Howard Baker of Tennessee (left) and Senator Sam Ervin of North Carolina (center).*

SATURDAY NIGHT LIVE APPEARS

NBC's Saturday Night Live began its run on 11 October 1975 as a freewheeling 90-minute comedy-variety show at the unheard-of hour of 11:30 EDT on Saturday nights. That should have sealed its doom, but it turned out to be the boldest leap in television comedy since Sid Caesar and Imogene Coca began *Your Show of Shows.*

Regular segments on the show have included the news satire 'Weekend Update,' the problems of the aliens on 'The Coneheads,' the Oriental swordsman 'Samurai Warrior' and 'The Blues Brothers.' Each program featured a guest host, and they came from all levels of public life – Ralph Nader, Julian Bond, George Carlin, Candice Bergen, Lily Tomlin, Richard Dreyfuss, New York Mayor Ed Koch, Fran Tarkenton, Ron Nessen and 80-year-old Mrs Miskel Spillman, who won an 'Anyone Can Host' write-in contest.

Countless *Saturday Night Live* alumni went on to greater fame in both television and the movies. Among them were Chevy Chase, John Belushi, Dan Aykroyd, Gilda Radner, Jane Curtin, Bill Murray, Joe Piscopo, Eddie Murphy, Tim Kazurinsky, Jim Belushi, Billy Crystal and Rich Hall.

Throughout its entire run, the show has featured fresh, often outrageous comedy and the excitement of bringing live television to late night viewers by 'The Not Ready for Prime Time Players,' a repertory company of wacky comics.

Above: *The Coneheads, Prymaat (Jane Curtin) and Beldaar (Dan Aykroyd).*

Right: *A 'Weekend Update' segment of a* Saturday Night Live *show. Left to right: John Belushi, Jane Curtin, Bill Murray and Don Novello as Father Guido Sarducci.*
Left: *The original cast of* NBC's Saturday Night Live *were Garrett Morris and Laraine Newman (bottom steps), John Belushi (top steps), Chevy Chase (left), Gilda Radner (standing on steps), and Jane Curtin and Dan Aykroyd (right) – the 'Not Ready for Prime Time Players.'*
Above: *Eddie Murphy plays a homosexual ladies' hair dresser in a* Saturday Night Live *skit.*

THE INSANE ENSEMBLE PROGRAM

Monty Python's Flying Circus was produced for the BBC and aired in Great Britain from 1969 to 1971, but was not available in the United States until 1974 and was first shown on a Texas PBS station. It was a half-hour of madness featuring skits (filmed or videotaped), blackouts and animated sequences. Often these were vaguely unified by a common comic thread, such as 'sex' or 'birdwatching.'

The characters were the thing — lecherous marriage counselors, nit-witted custom guards, idiotic farmers, upper-class morons, bumbling police constables. Boring talk shows and pretentious television documentaries were favorite targets, as were inane variety shows and stupid game shows. This PBS program had many moments of inspired madness, as when the British government created a Minister of Silly Walks, or when a *blanc mange* dessert won a tennis tournament or when people were mysteriously changed into Scotsmen and headed for the border.

The troupe was composed of six young men, Graham Chapman, John Cleese, Eric Idle, Terry Jones and Michael Palin. The nonspeaking member, and the only American of the group, was Terry Gilliam, who also designed the outrageous animated sequences.

The Monty Python group later went on to make many films together (and separately). These included such comedies as *Monty Python and the Holy Grail, The Life of Brian* and *Monty Python's The Meaning of Life.*

Above: *Left to right: Michael Palin, Graham Chapman, John Cleese and Eric Idle. The other sketch performer shown is not Terry Gilliam in disguise.*
Right: *On one of the skits on Monty Python's Flying Circus Hell's Grannies, a group of elderly women terrify the neighborhood with their acts of theft and violence.*
Left: *Monty Python's Flying Circus (left to right) John Cleese (with parrot), Terry Gilliam (with umbrella), Terry Jones (in drag), Graham Chapman (in uniform), Michael Palin (as Fred Gumby) and Eric Idle (in leopard skin).*

THE FIRST SYNDICATED SOAP OPERA

Mary Hartman, Mary Hartman was a comedy soap opera spoof that was designed for syndication, beginning in January 1976 and lasting for 325 half-hour episodes. The problems that the characters faced were more than any human could bear. Developed by Norman Lear (of *All In the Family* fame), it told of Mary Hartman (Louise Lasser), a 'typical American housewife' in the town of Fernwood, Ohio.

Pigtailed and plain, she went through one crisis after another. Her father (Philip Bruns) disappeared, her daughter (Claudia Lamb) was held prisoner by a mass murderer, her husband (Greg Mullavey) was impotent, her best friend (Mary Kay Place) was paralyzed, her grandfather (Victor Kilian) became known as the Fernwood Flasher for exposing himself, she had a nervous breakdown and an affair with a policeman (Bruce Solomon), her sister (Debralee Scott) became a hooker, her mother (Dody

Above: *Louise Lasser was the long-suffering Mary, and Greg*

Mullavey was her impotent husband.

Goodman) was flaky, and she was worried about how to avoid 'dirty yellow buildup' on her kitchen floor.

When Louise Lasser left the show in 1977, it continued for another six months under the title, *Forever Fernwood*. Most of the original cast was intact, but Tab Hunter had replaced Philip Bruns as Mary's father, the explanation being that George had fallen into a chemical vat and had been restored with plastic surgery. Also in the cast were Martin Mull, Dabney Coleman and Shelley Berman.

THE MOST WIDELY-VIEWED SERIES

More people saw *The Muppet Show* on syndication than any other series in history – some 235 viewers in more than 100 countries. It was produced from 1976 to 1981, and a total of 120 episodes were taped. Originated by an American, Jim Henson, and produced in England, the master of ceremonies was a frog named Kermit – not a real frog, but a puppet, or, as Henson called his menagerie, a Muppet. Other Muppets in the cast were Miss Piggy, Fozzie Bear, Gonzo, The Swedish Chef, Animal, Statler and Waldorf and many more.

The program was a half-hour of chaos, featuring such skits as 'Pigs in Space,' in which handsome Captain Link Heartthrob of the starship *Swinetrek* fought off the evil plots of Dr Strangepork and the advances of Miss Piggy. The humor was corny, but the Muppets themselves were appealing – they may have looked strange, but they were almost human.

Each week there was a guest star, and show business personalities were delighted to appear with these little creatures. Some of them were George Burns, Zero Mostel, Steve Martin, and even Rudolf Nureyev (who danced a *pas de deux* from 'Swine Lake' with Miss Piggy. Elton John (singing a song called 'Crocodile Rock' with a chorus of Muppet crocodiles) and Peter Sellers (as a mad German chiropractor tying a pig in knots) were also guests on the show.

Henson first approached ABC to do the show, but the people there thought it was just for kids. They were wrong.

Right: *Kermit the Frog and Miss Piggy on* The Muppet Show.
Far right top: *Guest Mark*

Hamill and the Muppets in Star Wars.
Far right bottom: *Jim Henson and friends.*

THE MOST WIDELY-VIEWED MINISERIES

Roots was a television adaptation of the book of the same name by Alex Haley in which he traced his own roots back to Africa and told of the capture of Kunta Kinte (Haley's ancestor), his being sent to America as a slave, and what happened to his progeny. The miniseries was one of the most remarkable achievements in the history of television, running for twelve hours and being broadcast on ABC for eight consecutive nights from 23 to 30 January 1977. It was the highest-rated series of all time, and all eight telecasts ranked among the 13th highest-rated single programs of all time. Some 130 million people in the United States watched at least part of *Roots*. It was nominated for three dozen Emmys and won them for Outstanding Limited Series, Outstanding Lead Actor for a Single Apperance (Louis Gossett Jr), Outstanding Single Performance by a Supporting Actor (Ed Asner), Outstanding Single Performance by a Supporting Actress (Olivia Cole), Outstanding Directing in a Drama Series (David Greene) and Outstanding Writing in a Drama Series (Ernest Kinoy and William Blinn).

In addition to Gossett, Asner and Cole, the cast included LeVar Burton as the young Kunta Kinte, John Amos, Cecily Tyson, Maya Angelou, O J Simpson, Moses Gunn, Ralph Waite, Lorne Greene, Lynda Day George, Vic Morrow, Robert Reed, Raymond St Jacques, Chuck Connors, Sandy Duncan, Leslie Uggams, Macdonald Carey, Scatman Crothers, George Hamilton, Carolyn Jones, Ben Vereen, Lloyd Bridges and Burl Ives.

Roots was so successful that producer David Wolper made a sequel bringing the history of the Haley family up to the present day, through the author's search for his family's past. *Roots: The Next Generation* was shown for seven consecutive nights in 1979, and featured such stars as Henry Fonda, Richard Thomas, Olivia de Havilland, Harry Morgan, Ruby Dee, Marlon Brando and James Earl Jones as Alex Haley.

Above: *John Amos as the older Kunte Kinte and Madge Sinclair as Bell.*

Below: *LeVar Burton (center) as the young Kinte aboard the slave ship.*

THE CAMP DAVID ACCORDS

On 19 November 1977, in a historic journey to promote Middle East Peace, Egyptian President Anwar Sadat traveled to Jerusalem at the invitation of Israeli Prime Minister Menachem Begin. It was the first time since the creation of the state of Israel in 1947 that an Egyptian leader had met with an Israeli leader on Israeli soil. The Arab states condemned Sadat's initiative, and he, in turn, broke diplomatic ties with Syria, Iraq, Libya, Algeria and South Yemen.

The time was ripe for a formal peace between Israel and Egypt, and it was President Jimmy Carter who took the initiative. All the television networks covered the historic Camp David Meetings of the three world leaders. On 17 September 1978, these private talks mediated by Carter culminated in the Camp David Accords between Sadat and Begin, establishing a time-table for peace negotiations.

On 26 March 1979, again with television cameras present, Sadat and Begin signed a peace treaty ending nearly 31 years of war. The other Arab nations, as well as the Palestine Liberation Organization, denounced the pact and imposed an economic boycott on Egypt, severing all diplomatic ties with Cairo.

As a result of this accord, Sadat and Begin shared the Nobel Prize for Peace in 1978.

Anwar Sadat of Egypt, President Jimmy Carter of the US and Menachem Begin of Israel at Camp David.

WHO SHOT J.R.?

Dallas premiered on CBS on 2 April 1978 and has been running ever since. It tells the story of the Ewing clan, an incredibly rich Texas family, and in the beginning there were in the family John Ross 'Jock' Ewing (Jim Davis), the head of the empire; Eleanor Southworth 'Miss Ellie' Ewing (Barbara Bel Geddes), his wife; and their three sons, Bobby (Patrick Duffy), Gary (David Ackroyd) and John Ross 'J.R.' Ewing Jr (Larry Hagman). J.R., the eldest, was the one that viewers loved to hate – a power-hungry, unscrupulous, conniving man who was continually unfaithful to his wife, Sue Ellen (Linda Gray).

At the end of the second season, the last original episode that year aired and J.R. (whom *Time* magazine had called 'that human oil slick') was shot by an unknown assailant and rushed to the hopsital in critical condition. All summer long, *Dallas* fans all over the world wondered who had shot him – there were at least 15 different people currently on the show who had legitimate motives. Bookies took in millions of dollars in wagers.

Finally, on 21 November 1980, the world found out. It was Kristin Shepard (Mary Crosby). She was pregnant with J.R.'s child, he ordered her to get out of town, and, when she refused, he was about to frame her on a charge of prostitution. Nearly 80 percent of all viewers in the United States who were watching television that night were tuned to *Dallas*.

Above: *Bobby Ewing (Patrick Duffy) and his wife Pam (Victoria Principal) are the most likeable members of the family.*
Right: *The second wedding of J R Ewing (Larry Hagman) and Sue Ellen (Linda Gray).*
Top right: *Larry Hagman on* Dallas, *as J R Ewing, 'the man you love to hate.'*

THE ATTEMPTED ASSASSINATION

On 30 March 1981, President Ronald Reagan was shot. He had just finished giving a speech at the Washington Hilton Ballroom and was walking toward his limousine just outside the hotel exit when John W Hinckley Jr stepped through a crowd of reporters and began firing his 22-caliber handgun. Three other people were hit by the shower of bullets, including Reagan's press secretary, James S Brady.

As police wrestled the gun from Hinckley, the president was rushed to George Washington University Hospital where he was treated for a possible lung collapse and went into surgery. Miraculously, none of the four men was killed. Brady was shot in the forehead and suffered extensive damage to his brain tissue, but ultimately lived.

All three major networks had photographers and reporters at the scene, and it was a matter of minutes before the story was shown on television – action film and all. Shortly thereafter, the three network anchormen were on

Above: *Police and Secret Service Men go after John W Hinckley Jr, after his assassination attempt on*

President Ronald Reagan.
Top: *Reagan leaves the Washington Hilton just before the shooting.*

the job, reporting to the nation about how the president and the other men were faring. Probably the most touching moment came when an erroneous report of Brady's death arrived at the ABC desk, and Brady's friend, newscaster Frank Reynolds, came close to bursting into tears.

THE BRITISH ROYAL WEDDINGS

Despite the American Revolution, and the 200 years since, many Americans have a warm spot in their hearts for the British Royal Family. That this is so, is revealed by the number of viewers whenever some Royal Occasion is televised. Americans were among the 500 million viewers of the Investiture of Prince Charles in 1969, and the 530 million who watched the wedding of Princess Anne and Captain Mark Phillips in 1977.

All three of the major networks expected similar interest in the wedding of Prince Charles to Lady Diana Spencer 29 July 1981, and sent their morning news teams to London for the entire week to follow the festivities, including full coverage of the actual wedding on Wednesday. And they were right, millions of Americans (of an estimated 750 million) began watching at 4:30 AM as the first of the state landaus bearing members of the Royal Family approached St Paul's Cathedral, and stayed glued to their sets as the bride, accompanied by her father set off in the traditional glass coach, used by George V at his Coronation in 1910. The ceremony, conducted by the Archbishop of Canterbury, with prayers by the heads of other churches in Great Britain including the Catholic Cardinal Archbishop of Westminster and the Moderator of the General Assembly of the Church of Scotland, was given a lovely air of reality when the bride spoke her husband's names in the wrong order. The new couple returned to the palace for the reception and to appear on the balcony to greet the waiting public, including the millions of television viewers.

At the wedding of Prince Andrew to Sarah Ferguson at Westminster Abbey on 29 July 1986, again the American networks took part, and once more many Americans were counted among 350 million viewers.

Above: *The new Duke and Duchess of York, Prince Andrew and the former Sarah Ferguson, wave to the crowd after their wedding at Westminster Abbey, 29 July 1986.*

Top: *The Prince and Princess of Wales return to Buckingham Palace.*
Right: *During the marriage service at the wedding of Prince Charles and Lady Diana.*

THE LAST BARNEY MILLER EPISODE

Barney Miller, starring Hal Linden in the title role, premiered on 23 January 1975 to mixed reviews. It told the story of a multi-ethnic band of officers in the 12th Precinct station house in New York City, and in its first season was almost axed by ABC. It was, however, a show that grew on the audience and lasted for seven years. The locale was the detective room on the second floor of a police station in Greenwich Village where Barney and his motley crew (and even more motley group of criminals and victims) spent their time.

When it came time to close up the precinct on television, the stage was set in the next to last episode. An antique gun was discovered in the precinct house and this revealed that the building had been Theodore Roosevelt's headquarters when he was President of the New York Police board in the 1890s. The building was declared a historical landmark and the men were to be transferred to a new station.

Top: *Detective Stanley 'Wojo' Wojohowicz (Maxwell Gail), Officer Carl Levitt (Ron Carey) and Captain Barney Miller (Hal Linden) in a scene from* Barney Miller.

In the final episode, 9 September 1982, Barney gets the phone call – he has been made deputy inspector, but the crew will be scattered to different locations throughout the city. Officer Carl Levitt (Ron Carey), Detective Stanley 'Wojo' Wojohowicz (Maxwell Gail), Detective Ron Harris (Ron Glass) and Detective Arthur Dietrich (Steve Landesberg) invite Barney out for a beer, but he stays in the deserted squad room and remembers (through flashbacks) the departed officers – Chano, Nick and Fish – a most moving experience.

NUCLEAR CONTROVERSY

Almost from the moment ABC announced that they would premiere a made-for-television movie called *The Day After* on 20 November 1983, arguments began concerning the wisdom of such a production. Made in the city of Lawrence, Kansas, the film told of the devastation caused by an all-out nuclear attack on a middle-sized American town. It was rather mild in terms of blood and gore, but conservatives attacked the motion picture as a threat to the United State's nuclear arms debate with the Soviets. Indeed, Secretary of State George P Shultz was given time to appear on ABC to present the Reagan Administration's side of the debate.

Long before the showing on television, hundreds of residents of Lawrence were treated to three free screenings

in mid-October, and did not seem too much affected. Still, all over the country, superintendents of schools set up educational meetings to discuss how principals and teachers would prepare their students for the broadcast. Then came the fateful night and more than 100 million Americans watched the tube – more than one-half of the country's adult population.

The program turned out to be less shocking than had been expected, and nuclear experts pointed out that the destruction had been actually soft-pedaled. Later that year and into the next, the film was shown in movie theaters throughout the world. Although Poland banned it for a few months, and the Japanese were naturally upset, it seemed not to be the shocker that had been expected in other lands, either.

Below: *Atomic destruction as seen on* The Day After.

THE LAST M*A*S*H EPISODE

*M*A*S*H* was something completely different – a comedy about war. Probably at any other time in the nation's history, such a program would not have worked. But when it premiered on 17 September 1972, the United States was embroiled in the lingering war in Vietnam. The climate created by this unpopular conflict made things seem right to tell the story of the 4077th Mobile Army Surgical Hospital during the Korean conflict – another unpopular 'police action.'

The job of the 4077th was to conduct 'meatball surgery' and to save as many wounded as possible. The doctors were depressed by the futility of patching up a soldier only to have him sent back to the front lines, the horrible living conditions in the field, and the general insanity of the war. Naturally, the only thing they could do was laugh. This truly was the first sitcom to use black humor.

Wisely the people behind the CBS show decided to end the series while it was still popular. The final episode, titled 'Goodbye, Farewell and Amen,' a two-and-a-half hour special, was aired on 28 February 1983, the last of 251 episodes during the show's 11 seasons. It drew a 77 share, meaning that 77 percent of all people watching television were watching *M*A*S*H*. By the end of the episode, the war was over. Alan Alda, the star, called it 'a long piece . . . in which the people say goodbye to each other and the experience. I think that the audience . . . deserves that kind of conclusion.'

Above: *B J Hunnicut (Mike Farrell), Margaret 'Hot Lips' Houlihan (Loretta Swit) and Hawkeye Pierce (Alan Alda) in M*A*S*H.*
Below: *Loading a time capsule* *in the last half-hour episode.*
Right top: *Pierce is helped out of his mental breakdown by Houlihan and Dr Sidney Freedman (Alan Arbus).*

Below: M*A*S*H *stars Alan Alda, David Ogden Stiers, Jamie Farr and William Christopher.*

THE COSBY SHOW

Almost from the beginning, television had run situation comedies that starred blacks, but they tended to be either patronizing (*Amos 'n' Andy, Beulah*) or rowdy and loud (*The Jeffersons, Good Times*). Then, on 20 September 1984, came *The Cosby Show*, the first sitcom to feature a middle-class black family. It was a gentle program about a busy New York obstetrician, Dr Heathcliff 'Cliff' Huxtable (Bill Cosby), his lawyer wife, Clair (Phylicia Ayers-Allen Rashad), and their five children. Sondra (Sabrina LeBeauf), age 20, was off in college. Denise (Lisa Bonet), age 16, and Theodore, usually called 'Theo' (Malcolm Jamal Warner), age 14, were the know-it-all teenagers. Vanessa (Tempestt Bledsoe), age 8, was the rambunctious one. And Ruby (Keshia Knight Pulliam), age 5, was the adorable little girl who always said the wrong thing.

This family comedy hinged on the trials and tribulations of Cliff and Clair as they tried to raise their family while maintaining their own active professional lives. Some of the everyday problems were the kids' puppy loves, grandparents who meddled, the selection of birthday presents, difficulties at school and sibling rivalry.

The program turned out to be the sleeper of NBC's 1984 lineup, and soon became the top-rated show in the ratings because it was a program that everyone felt akin to with sympathetic characters.

LIVE AID

One of the most highly publicized and successful special programs of 1985 was the Live Aid Concert of July 13. Hundreds of rock-and-roll musicians gathered at John F Kennedy Stadium in Philadelphia and Wembley Stadium in London to give a marathon concert to raise money for famine victims in Africa. The concert, simulcast on television and radio, featured a live hookup between the United States and Great Britain, and was also broadcast and telecast live around the world.

Some 90,000 spectators in Philadelphia and 72,000 in London made up the live audience, and some 1.9 billion people in 150 countries heard the concert, or part of it, on radio or saw it on television. By the midpoint of the day, more than $20 million had been promised through telephone pledges. At the end of the show it was estimated that $70 million would have been raised, and Bob Geldof, the coordinator of the concert, promised that 100 percent of the money raised would go to African Relief.

The Nielsen ratings for the concert were quite good. Although it ranked 30th out of 64 programs in the week of July 8-14, it was seen, at least in part, by 40 million Americans, and no one could estimate how many heard some of it on radio.

Top right: *Bill Cosby, the star of* The Cosby Show.
Far right top: *The* Live Aid *finale from London's Wembley Stadium, with Bob Geldof, Paul McCartney and David Bowie.*

Far right bottom: *The singers in Philadelphia led by Harry Belafonte and Lionel Ritchie rejoice.*
Right: Live Aid *from JFK Stadium in Philadelphia.*

THE CHALLENGER TRAGEDY

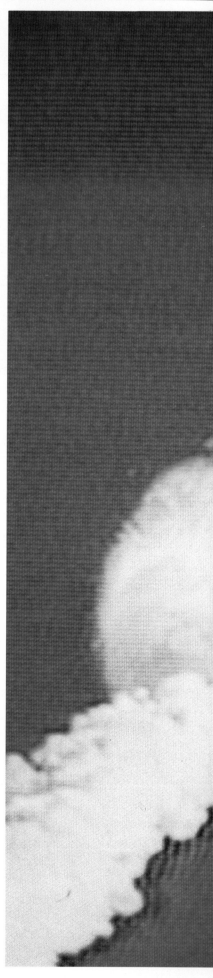

By 28 January 1986, space launches had become so commonplace that the three major networks had decided not to cover the blastoff of the *Challenger* space shuttle flight that day. Only Ted Turner's Cable Network News (CNN) was on hand to record the events of the flight when the unthinkable happened, 73.631 seconds after liftoff, and millions of television viewers saw the horrible explosion that took the lives of the seven crew members.

The people on board were: Christa McAuliffe, a New Hampshire school teacher, who was to have been the first civilian in space; Air Force Major Francis R Scobee, the commander of the *Challenger*; Judith Resnick, a payload specialist with a PhD in electrical engineering; Ronald McNair, also a payload specialist, the black astronaut with a doctorate in physics; Naval Commander Michael Smith, a pilot-astronaut; Air Force Major Ellison Onizuka, the payload specialist who was a former test pilot for the US Air Force; and Gregory Jarvis, a satellite engineer representing Hughes Aircraft, who was also trained as an astronaut. About one minute after liftoff, the ground controllers informed the crew that they were 'go for throttle up.' The last words from the *Challenger* crew that were heard in Mission Control were Francis R 'Dick' Scobee's, 'Roger, go for throttle up,' and then, about two-tenths of a second before the explosion, Smith's 'Uh-oh.'

CNN had sent a crew to Mrs McAuliffe's school to get reactions from her students about what was supposed to be a normal, no-problem flight. The TV pictures of their looks of horror when the *Challenger* exploded will never be forgotten. Television had, once again, brought history into the lives of the viewers.

Above: *The fated members of the Space Shuttle 51-L. Seated, from left: Michael Smith, Francis 'Dick' Scobee, Ronald McNair. Back, from left: Ellison Onizuka, Christa McAuliffe, Greg Jarvis, Judy Resnik.*
Right: *On 28 January 1986, the space shuttle* Challenger *lifted off from Cape Canaveral with its crew of seven aboard. Space launches had become so common that only CNN – the Cable News Network – was covering the story. Seventy-three seconds later, millions of television viewers saw the tragic explosion.*

Adams, Edie 34, 59
Admiral Broadway Revue 18
Agnew, Spiro T 99, *99*
Alda, Alan 74, 122, *122, 123*
Aldrin, Edwin E (Buzz) 95
Alexander, Ben 38
All in the Family 20, 104, *104*
Allen, Fred 26, 78
Allen, Steve 26, 52, 63
Allison, Fran 14, 15
Amahl and the Night Visitors 39, 59
American Bandstand 59
Amos, John 114, *114*
Andrews, Julie *58*, 59
Arms, Russell 31
Armstrong Circle Theatre 14, 25
Armstrong, Neil A 95
Arnaz, Desi 23, 36
Arness, James 54, *54*
Aykroyd, Dan *108, 109, 109*

Baker, Senator Howard *106, 107*
Ball, Lucille 23, 36
Barney Miller 120, *120*
Batman 80, *80, 81, 82-83*
Beatles, The 57, 75
Begin, Menachim 115, *115*
Bel Geddes, Barbara 116
Belushi, John *108, 109, 109*
Bendix, William 20
Berg, Gertrude 16, 17
Berle, Milton 41, 80
Blake, Amanda 54, *54*
Bowie, David 125, *125*
Bradley, Ed 94, *94*
Brady, James S 114
Brinkley, David 24
Broadway Open House 27
Brokaw, Tom 41
Burton, Le VAr 114, *114*

CBS Evening News 94
Caesar, Sid *6*, 18-19, 109
Camel News Caravan 24
Captain Video and his Video Rangers 20
Carey, Ron 120, *120*
Carson, Johnny 35
Carter, President Jimmy 12, 115, *115*
Cerf, Bennett 26
Chancellor, John 41, 95
Chapman, Graham 110, *111*
Charlie Brown Christmas, A 77, *77*
Chase, Chevy *108*, 109
Child, Julia 69, *69*
Cinderella 59
Clark, Dick 20, 59
Cleese, John 110, *110, 111*
Coca, Imogene *6*, 18-19, 109
Cole, Olivia 114, *114*
Collins, Dorothy 30
Collins, Michael 95
Cosby, Bill 77, *77*, 124, *124*
Cosby Show, The 124, *124*
Cousin Bette 102, *103*
Cronkite, Walter 14, 71, 88, 94, 99
Crusader Rabbit 25
Culp, Robert 77, *77*
Cunningham, Ronnie 19
Curtin, Jane *108, 109, 109*
Cypher, Jon *58*, 59

Dallas 116, *116*
Daly, John Charles 26
Day After, The 121, *121*
De Lugg, Milton 27, 31
Desmond, Johnny 31
Ding Dong School 44
Dodd, Jimmy 54
Downs, Hugh 41, 52
Dragnet 38
Duffy, Patrick 116, *116*

Ed Sullivan Show, The 57, 75

Ed Wynn Show, The 23
Elizabeth II 46
Ernie Kovacs Show, The 34
Ervin, Senator Sam *106*, 107
Evans, Maurice 44

Faraway Hill 12
Farrell, Mike 122, *122*
First Churchills, The 102, *102*
Ford, President Gerald 12, 107
Forsyte Saga, The 98
Francis, Arlene 26
Frawley, William 36
French Chef, The 69
Frost, David 74
Funicello Annette 54

Gail, Maxwell 120, *120*
Garland, Judy 78
Garroway, Dave 26, 41
Geldof, Bob 1, 124
Gibson, Henry 87
Gillespie, Darlene 54
Gilliam, Terry 110, *110*
Gleason, Jackie 13, 20, 57
Glenn, John 66
Goldbergs, The 16, 17
Goodman, Dody 52, 112
Gray Linda 116, *116*
Gumbel, Bryant 41
Gunsmoke 54

Hagman, Larry 116, *116*
Hallmark Hall of Fame 39, 41
Hamlet 44
Hammerstein, Oscar II 29, 59
Hampshire, Susan 98, 102, *102*
Hastings, Don 20
Hayes, Helen 30
Hector, Louis 9, 10
Henderson, Skitch 52
Henson, Jim 101, 112, *113*
Herbert, Don 32
Horwich, Dr Frances 44
Howard, Leslie 10, 11
Howdy Doody 26, 63
Humphrey, Hubert H 98, *93*
Huntley-Brinkley Report, The 25
Huntley, Chet 24

I Love Lucy 36
I Spy 77, *77*
Idle, Eric 110, *110, 111*

Jack Parr Show, the 52
Jarvis, Gregory 126, *126*
Johnson, Arte, *86*, 87
Johnson, President Lyndon B 64, 71, 88
Jones, Terry 110, *110*
Judy Garland Show, The 78

Kefauver, Estes 33
Kelley, DeForest 85, *85*
Kennedy, Jacqueline *64*, 71, *71, 72, 73*
Kennedy, President John F 62, *64*, 68, 70, 70-73
Kilgallen, Dorothy 26, 52
King, Dr Martin Luther 68, *69*, 92, *92*
Koenig, Walter *84, 85, 85*
Kovacs, Ernie 34, 52
Kuhlman, Rosemary 39
Kukla, Fran and Ollie 14, 26

Lanson, Snooky 30
Lasser, Louise 112, *112*
Leonard, Jack E 27
Lester, Jerry 27
Life Is Worth Living 41
Life of Riley, The 20
Linden, Hal 120, *120*
Lindsay, Howard *58*, 59
Live Aid 124, *124*
Loeb, Philip 17

*M*A*S*H* 38, 122
MacKenzie, Gisele 31
Manzano, Sonia 100, 101
March, Hal 53
Marin, Dick *86, 87, 87*
Martin, Mary 48
Marx, Groucho 29
Massey, Raymond 11, 30
Masterpiece Theatre 98, 102-103
McAuliffe, Christa 126, *126*
McCarthy, Senator Joseph 12, 49, 51
McGee, Frank 41, 62, 71
McGrath, Bob *100*, 101
McKay, Jim 105, *105*
McMahon, Ed 53
McNair, Ronald 126, *126*
McQuaid, Arlene 16, 17
Meet The Press 12
Melendez, Bill 77
Menotti, Gian-Carlo 13, 39
Meredith, Burgess 60, 80
Merman, Ethel 78
Mickey Mouse Club, The 54
Miller, Mitch 64, *64*
Minnelli, Liza 78
Mintz, Eli 16, 17
Mr Wizard 26
More, Kenneth 98
Morgan, Harry 38, 114
Morris, Garrett *108*, 109
Mullavey, Grey 112, *112*
Murray, Bill 109, *109*
Murrow, Edward R 49

NBC Nightly News 25
Neville, John 102, *102*
Newman, Edwin R 41
Newman, Laraine *108*, 109
Nichols, Nichelle 85, *85*
Nimoy, Leonard *84, 85, 85*
Nixon, President Richard M 42, 62, 99, 107, *107*

O'Connor, Carroll 104, *104*
Onizuka, Ellison 126, *126*
Oz, Frank 101

Pagliacci 11
Palin, Michael 110, *110, 111*
Palmer, John 41
Paul Whitman's TV Teen Club 20
Pauley, Jane 41
Pennell, Nicholas 98
Perkins, Marlin 27
Peyton Place 12, 76, *76*
Porter, Eric 98
Porter, Nyree Dawn 98
Presley, Elvis 57, 59
Principal, Victoria 116, *116*
Pulitzer Prize Playhouse 30

Radner, Gilda *108*, 109
Radulovitch, Milo 49
Rather, Dan 71, 94
Ray, James Earl 92
Reagan, President Ronald 117, *117*
Reasoner, Harry 94, *94*
Red Skelton Show, The 35
Reiner, Rob 104, *104*
Remick, Lee 45
Resnick, Judith 126, *126*
Reynolds, Frank 68, 117
Robinson, Matt 101
Rocky and His Friends 25, *25*
Rodgers, Richard 29, 43, 59
Roots 114
Rountree, Martha 12
Rowan and Martin's Laugh-In *86, 87, 87*
Rowan, Dan *86, 87, 87*
Ruby, Jack 71
Rydell, Bobby 20, 59

Sadat, Anwar 115, *115*
Safer, Morley 94. *94*

Saturday Night Live 108, 109
Sawyer, Diane 94, *94*
Scarlet Pimpernel, The *10*, 11
Scobee, Francis R 126, *126*
Scott, Willard 41
Serling, Rod 60
Sesame Street 44, *100*, 101
Shalit, Gene 41
Shatner, William *84*, 85, *85*
Shepard, Alan B 6, 65
Sheen, Bishop Fulton J 41
Sing Along With Mitch 64
$64,000 Question 53
60 Minutes 94
Skelton, Red 35
Smith, Buffalo Bob 63
Smith, Howard K 62, 71
Smith, Michael 126, *126*
Spivak, Lawrence K 12
Stack, Robert 61
Stapleton, Jean 104, *104*
Star Trek *84-85*, 85
Stickney, Dorothy *58*, 59
Stone, Milburn 54, *54*
Storm, The 13
Struthers, Sally 104, *104*
Studio One 13
Sullavan, Margaret 13
Sullivan, Ed 52, 74
Swayze, John Cameron 24
Swit, Loretta *122, 123*

Takei, George 85, *85*
Texaco Star Theater 41
That Was The Week That Was 74, 87

Three Garridebs, The 9, 10
Tillstrom, Burr 14, 15, 74
Today Show, The 41, 53
Tomlin, Lily 87, 109
Tonight Show, The 27, 53, *53*
Truth or Consequences 28
Twenty-One 53
Twilight Zone, The 60
Tyzack, Margaret 98, *103*

Untouchables, The 61, *61*
Upstairs, Downstairs 102, 103

Van, Bobby 18, 19
Van Doren, Charles 53
Vance, Vivian 36
Victory At Sea 42

Wallace, Mike 13, 94, *94*
Ward, Burt 80, *80, 81, 82-83*
Watch Mr Wizard 32
Weaver, Dennis 54, *54*
Webb, Jack 38
Welles, Orson 45
West, Adam 80, *80, 81, 82-83*
What's My Line 26
Whiteman, Paul 20
Wickes, Mary 45
Wild Kingdom 27
Wynn, Ed 8, 23, 78

You Bet Your Life 29
Your Hit Parade 30
Your Show of Shows 18, 109

Zoo Parade 26

Acknowledgements
The author and publisher would like to thank the following people who have helped in the preparation of this book: Elizabeth Montgomery who edited it; Jean Chiaramonte Martin and Donna Cornell Muntz who did the picture research; Mike Rose who designed it, and Rick and Nancy Marschall who prepared the index.

Photo Credits
The Bettmann Archive Inc: pages 7 (right), 10, 13, 18-19, 19, 20, 23 (both), 24-5, 35 (top), 39 (bottom), 41 (top), 56-7, 58, 86, 113 (bottom), 116 (top).
The Billy Rose Theatre Collection, The New York Public Library at Lincoln Center: pages 9 (top), 12.
Bison Picture Library: pages 2 (top and bottom), 3 (top left), 4, 6 (top left), 26 (top), 30, 30-1, 36 (both), 37 (top), 54, 55, 59 (both), 60 (bottom), 61, 63 (both), 76, 77 (both), 78-9, 80, 81, 82-3, 84-5, 85, 87, 92 (top), 93 (both), 94 (top), 101 (both), 102-03, 103, 104 (top), 105 (top), 106, 108, 109 (all three), 110, 111 (both), 112, 112-13, 113 (top), 114 (both), 116 (bottom two), 120, 121, 122 (both), 123 (both), 124 (top).
Camera Press Ltd: page 98 (both).
Department of Defense: pages 88 (top), 89 (both), 91 (both).
Michael Evans/The White House: pages 115, 117 (both).
Hallmark Hall of Fame: pages 44 (bottom), 45 (both).
Lyndon Baines Johnson Library: page 71 (bottom).
John F Kennedy Library: pages 6 (top right) 64, 70, 72 (both), 73 (top and center).
Museum of Modern Art/Film Stills Archive: page 14 (top).
NASA: pages 67, 95, 96-7.
National Archives: pages 42-3, 43.
National Film Archive, London: pages 8-9.
New York Public Library: page 33 (bottom).
Nixon Presidential Materials Project, National Archives: 107.
Phototeque: pages 11, 14 (bottom), 37 (bottom), 41 (bottom), 53 (top), 57, 60 (top), 100, 105 (bottom).
RCA: page 9 (bottom).
Rex Features Ltd: page 102.
S & G Press Agency: pages 46, 46-7, 118 (both), 119.
Karl Schumacher/The White House: page 3 (top right).
Alex Siodmak: page 6 (bottom).
Springer/Bettmann Film Archive: pages 13, 15, 34, 48, 53 (bottom).
UPI/Bettmann Newsphotos: 2 (center), 7 (left), 33 (top), 42, 49 (both), 50-1, 51, 52 (top), 62, 65, 66, 68-9, 69 (both), 71 (top and center), 73 (bottom), 74-5, 92 (bottom), 94 (bottom), 99, 104 (bottom), 106-07, 124 (bottom), 125 (both), 126, 126-7.
US Navy: pages 88 (bottom), 90.
Wisconsin Center for Film and Theater Research: pages 12-13, 16, 17, 18, 21, 22 (both), 26 (bottom), 27, 28, 29, 32, 35 (bottom), 38, 39 (top), 40 (both), 44 (top), 52 (bottom), 64 (top), 74 (both).